the
Merli
tarot

the
Merlin
tarot

R J Stewart

ILLUSTRATED BY MIRANDA GRAY

Element
An Imprint of HarperCollins*Publishers*
77–85 Fulham Palace Road
Hammersmith, London W6 8JB

The website address is:
www.thorsonselement.com

and Element are trademarks of
HarperCollins*Publishers* Limited

First published by The Aquarian Press, 1992
This edition published by Element, 2003

1 3 5 7 9 10 8 6 4 2

A catalogue record of this book
is available from the British Library

ISBN 000 716562 5

Printed and bound in China

Contents

Illustrations

Introduction

This short handbook is designed to give you basic information on the Merlin Tarot. The deck has very individual Trump designs, and there are several unique methods of laying out the cards for meditation, visualization and divination. For a full study of the Merlin Tarot, and the history of how the deck was designed, you should read *The Complete Merlin Tarot*, a separate substantial book which deals in depth with every card of the deck. It also describes a wide range of uses for the deck, and many aspects of tarot (and of the Merlin tradition), which appear in the cards and related patterns or methods of use.

The Merlin Tarot comprises 22 Trumps, 40 Numbers and 16 Court cards or People, giving a deck of 78 cards. There are also 2 further cards with key figures for rapid reference while using the deck. The first of these, The Creation Vision, shows the sequence of Trumps from Earth to the Stars and back again, as follows:

1 The Moon   2 The Sun   3 The Star
(The Three Worlds)

4 Fortune   5 Justice   6 Judgement
(The Three Wheels)

7 The Fool   8 The Magician   9 The Chariot
(The Three Enlighteners)

10 The Guardian   11 The Blasted   12 Death
(The Three Liberators)   Tower

13 The Hanged Man   14 The Hermit   15 The Innocent
(The Three Redeemers)

16 Temperance   17 The Emperor 18 Strength
(The Three Givers)

19 The Empress   20 The Lovers   21 The Priestess
(The Three Sharers)

22 The Universe
(One Manifest Reality)

The card also shows the basic Tree of Life (see Figure 2, p.xi) and the simple planetary attributes of each Sphere of the Tree. Our Trump 21, for example, The Priestess, reveals the consciousness/energy of the Moon and Venus, of the emotions and the generative lunar powers. These attributes are described in detail in the summaries of each Trump, which appear in the order 1–22 beginning on p.1. (Please note that the numbering of the Merlin Tarot is purely for reference, and is not connected to the so-called 'traditional' numbering or order of tarot Trumps that appears in publication from the nineteenth century onwards. The difference between contrived literary systems of tarot correspondences and the perennial natural or holistic traditions is discussed in *The Complete Merlin Tarot.*)

The second reference card is The Two Dragons, an image drawn from the prophetic vision of the young Merlin, whose powers were awakened by the arousal of two dragons in the Underworld. This card shows the Trump relationships in a simpler form, as they relate to one another through the Three Worlds.

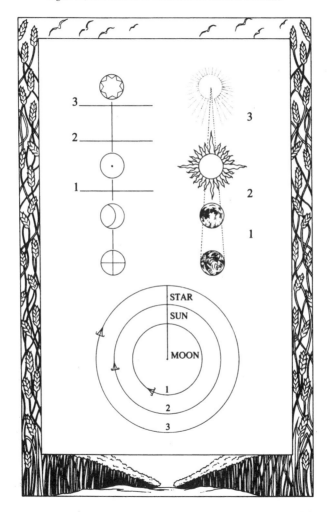

Working with the Deck

Whether you are already using tarot or are a complete beginner, the following sequence will be helpful in gaining a deeper understanding of the Merlin Tarot.

Figure 2: THE TREE OF LIFE

Spheres

1st:	*Primum Mobile*/Crown	
2nd:	The Zodiac/Wisdom	
3rd:	Understanding	♄
4th:	Mercy	♃
5th:	Severity	♂
6th:	Beauty	☉
7th:	Victory	♀
8th:	Honour	☿
9th:	Foundation	☽
10th:	Kingdom	⊕

Trumps or Paths

1: The Moon; 2: The Sun; 3: Star (The Three Worlds); 4: The Wheel of Fortune; 5: Justice; 6: Judgement (The Three Wheels); 7: The Fool; 8: The Magician; 9: The Chariot; 10: The Guardian; 11: The Blasted Tower; 12: Death; 13: The Hanged Man; 14: The Hermit (The Eight Ascending Images); 15: The Innocent; 16: Temperance; 17: The Emperor; 18: Strength; 19: The Empress; 20: The Lovers; 21: The Priestess; 22: The Universe (The Eight Descending Images).

NOTE: The Trump or Path numbers relate to the cycle of ascent and descent (see p.1). They are not related to mystical numerology or alphabetic correspondences.

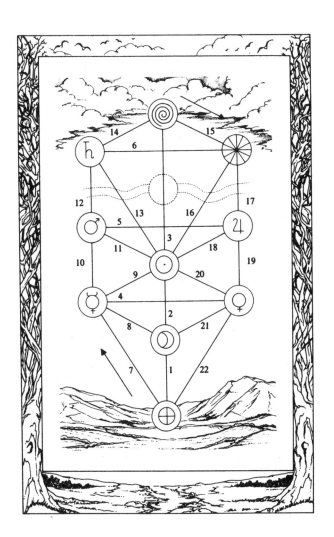

If you want to get the best from this deck, do not rush into divination by looking up 'meanings' in this handbook or in the larger book written for the complete deck. The meanings must come from *within ourselves*, and not mechanically from reference sources. The following method, which does not take a lot of time, is the best way towards using the deck. It is designed to give you insights long before you use the cards for divination, and will empower any divinatory work that you undertake. Divination is a lesser art of tarot, the great arts being meditation and visualization, particularly with the powerful Trumps.

The Trumps, Wheels and Worlds

The first helpful way of working with the deck is simply to lay the Trumps out in the order shown in the two reference cards. You will find a harmony, a living pattern, in this. It reveals the *energies* from Earth to the stars, those same energies as they resonate within each of us, and their collective or ancestral pattern. The Merlin Tarot and tradition is based upon the idea of Sacred Space, with all energies and consciousness turning about the Three Worlds of Moon, Sun and Star. The three octaves or three turns of the spiral from Earth to stars are represented by the Three Wheels of Fortune, Justice and Judgement (see Figures 1 and 7, pp.ix and 52).

The next stage is to meditate upon each Trump separately, in the order shown. You will see that they fit in pairs, triads and groups of relationships of various kinds (see Figures 2 and 4, pp.xi and 2). Try to feel these patterns within yourself, try to see them in the environment from land to sky, Earth to stars. They are part of our consciousness and energy, the Microcosm, and part of the greater worlds of the planet, solar system, and universe, the Macrocosm. The two mirror one another.

At all stages, refer to the various illustrations, and try always to lay out cards in the patterns shown. Our own energies and relative position as humans upon the planet are represented by the Seven Directions (see Figure 5, p.48): if you work with this concept, it comes alive, and the tarot cards achieve new depths of resonance and meaning when they are returned to their primal order based upon Moon, Sun and Star.

The Numbers

Once you have become familiar with the Trump patterns, begin to work through the Number cards. There are four suits, one for each Element (Air, Fire, Water and Earth), from Ace to Ten. The summary of the numbers is found in Chapter 2.

If you lay the Number cards out around the Wheel of Life (Figure 6, p.49), you will discover how they relate to one another. You will also see that certain numbers relate to certain Trumps, as shown upon the Tree of Life (Figure 2). Trump 3, The Star, for example, has affinity with the Four Aces and the Four Sixes, for it reveals the powers of the 1st and 6th Spheres, the Crown of Stars and the Sun of Beauty. Trump 7, The Fool, has affinity with the Four Eights and the Four Tens, and so forth.

You can also lay the Number cards out according to the Tree of Life, from the Four Aces at the Crown to the Four Tens in the Kingdom. When setting the Number cards out in this pattern, lay the relevant Trumps between them as shown in our key cards and various figures. This will show how the entire deck begins to relate throughout.

The Court Cards or People

The 16 Court cards can now be approached. (The summary of the Courts is found in Chapter 3.)

Lay them out according to the Court Circle (Figure 15, p.92) and meditate upon their relationship to one another and to the Four Elements, Seasons and Directions around the Wheel of Life (Figure 6, p.49).

The wheel or circle of Court cards can also be laid out around any of the Three Wheels and Worlds, with the Court of Birds or Air at the crown, Serpents or Fire at the right, Fishes or Water below and Beasts or Earth at the left. Try laying them around each of the Three Wheels and Worlds in turn. Finally, assemble the entire universe of Trumps and Number cards according to the Dragons (Tree of Life) and then add the Courts: Air at the top of the Tree, Fire to the right, Water beneath, Earth to the left. Meditate upon this pattern and its holism of relationships.

You may also work with the Court cards by relating them to the central Spheres of the *Axis Mundi* or Tree of Life: Earth, Moon, Sun and Crown. Planet Earth has the Court of Earth/Beasts rotating around it, the planetary Moon has the Court of Water/Fishes, the Sun has the Court of Fire/Serpents, and the Crown has the Court of Air/Birds. This pattern is shown in Figure 20, p.135.

Divination, Farsight and Insight

When you have worked through the patterns of layout, meditation, and vision briefly described above, you will find that divinatory work comes alive most powerfully, and you can work with the specific new layouts described in Chapter 4. At first, it will be necessary to refer to this handbook for summaries

Figure 3: THE CREATION VISION
(based on the Vita Merlini *and* Prophecies)

The First Wheel: The Lunar World – centred upon the Moon.

☉ Energy/spirit/transpersonal consciousness.
☽ Psyche/sexual energies/subconscious and collective or ancestral consciousness.
♀ Emotions.
☿ Intellect.
⊕ Body and outer events.

The Second Wheel: The Solar World – centred upon the Sun.

♌ The Abyss (crossed by Trumps 3, 13, 16).
☉ Transpersonal consciousness.
☽ Psyche, subconscious (supporting emotions and intellect).
♂ Catabolic energies/consciousness.
♃ Anabolic energies/consciousness.

The Third Wheel: The Stellar World – centred upon the unknown or void.

♅ *Primum Mobile*/seed of being.
♌ The Abyss or void.
☉ Transpersonal consciousness (source of lower consciousness).
♄ Universal Understanding.
♆ Universal Wisdom.

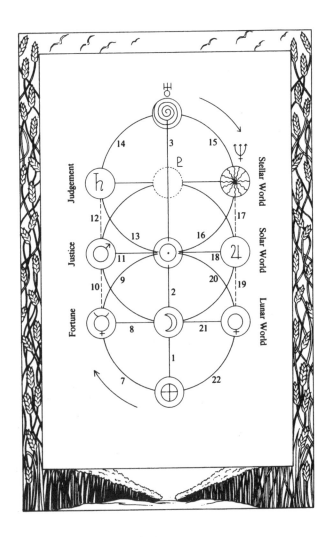

and attributes, or to the larger reference book *The Complete Merlin Tarot*. (As already mentioned, this second book contains much deep tarot lore and advanced work, as well as many insights into the basics that can only be touched upon in a short handbook.) You will need the summaries less and less, however, as you become more familiar with the Merlin Tarot.

The relationship between divination, farsight and insight is inherent in tarot, and a good tarot worker uses all three, but most of all he or she uses insight, working with the images to reveal truth. This may be truth about yourself, about a question, about other people or about a situation. In its true function and power, tarot tells the story of the Creation of the Worlds, so it reveals truths about powers, energies, consciousness and the countless patterns that combine and recombine to form our manifest world.

If you wish to find out more about the tradition, designs and intent of the Merlin Tarot before you work with it, please read the opening chapters of *The Complete Merlin Tarot*. Otherwise, we shall begin now with a summary of the Trumps in order from 1 to 22.

1

The Trumps

Summary of the Trumps

Arrange your Trumps in the order 1–22, as shown below and in Figures 3 and 4. When studying the summaries, have only each card before you in turn, rather than the entire 22. Read the summary, then spend some time in meditation upon the image itself and upon its key meanings and attributes.

This same simple method applies to the Number and Court cards. When you have worked through the Trumps, Number and Court cards in this way, begin working with them in pairs, triads and fourfold patterns, as seen in our various illustrations.

Figure 4: TRUMP RELATIONSHIPS: The Cycle of Ascent and Descent

Partners or polar pairs of Trumps					D
A	14	The Hermit – The Innocent	15	E
S	13	The Hanged Man – Temperance	16	S
C	12	Death – The Emperor	17	C
E	11	The Blasted Tower – Strength	18	E
N	10	The Guardian – The Empress	19	N
D	9	The Chariot – The Lovers	20	D
I	8	The Magician – The Priestess	21	I
N	7	The Fool – The Universe	22	N
G				G

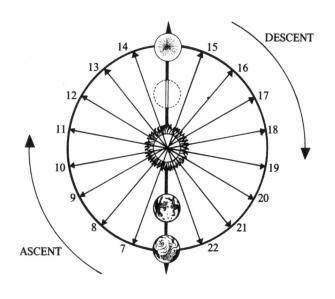

Ultimate or Extreme Pairs of Trumps

1
The Moon

World
The Lunar World, including planet Earth.

Wheel
The First Wheel, Fortune.

Beings
Spirits, *daemones*, ex-humans, elementals and nature spirits. Beings from other dimensions and worlds such as fairies or ancestral beings.

Consciousness
Human, ancestral and collective, personal or masked. The entire range of thought, emotion and energies within any entity, including dream consciousness and hidden realms of awareness within the psyche.

Partner Trumps
The Sun and Moon. Also polarized rotation of Trumps around the central Moon and connecting to Earth (see Figure 3).

Spheres and Planets
Spheres: The 9th and 10th Spheres, Foundation and Kingdom.
Planets: Luna and Earth.

Attributes
The lower third of the *Axis Mundi*, Middle Pillar or Spindle of Worlds. Life power in formation and expression. The Four Elements and their inner reflections of consciousness.

God and Goddess Forms
Luna and the Earth Mother. All goddesses of fertility, birth, life, death and nature. Also goddesses of prevision, prophecy and magical or supernatural practices.

Key Phrases
The Kingdom of Life/The foundation of power/passage of awareness inwards and outwards/reflection and reproduction/ the Mysteries behind Nature.

Merlin Texts[1]
PVM The Goddess of the Land; *VM* Description of Lunar World and its inhabitants, description of the Earth and its regions, energies, creatures and hidden dimensions.

Divinatory Meaning
Unconscious forces or unseen influences from within materialize into outer life. Matters relating to birth and death, dreams and desires. Collective or group modes of behaviour and awareness. May also indicate the early stages of inner transformation or initiation.

Related Number Cards
Nines and Tens (or Aces).
Nines: Misfortune, Endurance, Fulfilment, Means.
Tens: Disaster, Responsibility, Friendship, Opportunity.

---

[1] *H = The History of the Kings of Britain* (c. 1135), *PVM = The Prophetic Vision of Merlin* (*Prophecies*, c. 1135); *VM = The Mystic Life of Merlin* (*Vita Merlini*, c. 1150).

2
The Sun

World
The Solar World (crossing into the Lunar).

Wheel
The Second Wheel, Justice, *and* the Third Wheel, Fortune.

Beings
The Solar Entity (includes the planetary entities), Angels, Innerworld Masters and Saints, Illuminated Ones, transpersonal teachers and guides. Saviours and Redeemers in world religion and mystical comprehension.

Consciousness
Solar or central knowledge/transpersonal consciousness/illuminated awareness.

Partner Trumps
The Star above, The Moon below. The rotation of polarized Trumps located upon the solar or 6th Sphere (see Figures 1, 2 and 7).

Spheres and Planets
Spheres: The 6th and 9th Spheres, Beauty and Foundation.
Planets: Sol and Luna.

Attributes

The middle third of the *Axis Mundi*, Middle Pillar or Spindle of Worlds. Balance of Power in motion; full awareness and natural harmonious relationship of polarized energies. Arousal and direction of life forces from their origin. Creative consciousness.

God and Goddess Forms

The Son of Light and the Mother of Life/Mabon and Modron/Sol and Luna. All divine sons, children and their mothers.

Key Phrases

The equal light of Sun and Moon/perfected power/knowledge of life/central consciousness/the foundation of harmony.

Merlin Texts

H The young Merlin; *PVM* Vision of a rider upon a white horse who directs rivers; *VM* Description of the Solar World.

Divinatory Meaning

A powerful harmonizing, centralizing influence or energy upon life patterns. Emergence of new meaning, knowledge and higher levels of awareness within the inquirer. Creative adjustment of inner energies, movement towards transpersonal consciousness. General indication of positive, beneficial therapy both inwardly and outwardly.

Related Number Cards

Sixes and Nines.
Sixes: Transition, Balance, Joy, Benefit.
Nines: Misfortune, Endurance, Fulfilment, Means.

3
The Star

World
The Stellar World (crossing into the Solar).

Wheel
The Third Wheel, Judgement, (crossing the Second Wheel, Justice).

Beings
Stellar entities, Archangels. Originative Being.

Consciousness
Universal, transhuman, transcendent.

Partner trumps
Higher harmonic of The Sun and The Moon.

Spheres and Planets
Spheres: The 1st and 6th Spheres, Crown and Beauty.
Planets: The Pleiades and the sun; the sun as a star.

Attributes
The upper third of the *Axis Mundi*, Spindle or Middle Pillar of the Tree of Life; the ultimate pivot of universal consciousness; crossing the Abyss between the Stellar and Solar Worlds.

God and Goddess Forms
The Holy Spirit or First Breath *with* The Son of Light; Astraea or the Weaver of Stars *with* Apollo, Lugh, Belenos, Christ.

Key Phrases
Harmony of spirit/innermost light/universal truth/ knowledge of being/transcendent illumination/grace.

Merlin Texts
PVM: The goddess Ariadne who weaves stars; *VM:* Description of Stellar World and its inhabitants.

Divinatory Meaning
A profound spiritual impulse or transcendent energy at work, usually within the inquirer, but sometimes also within a personal situation involving the inquirer. May also mean a collective or cosmic energy pattern involving many people, including the inquirer.

Related Number Cards
Aces and Sixes.
Aces: Life, Light, Love and Law.
Sixes: Transition, Balance, Joy, Benefit.

4
The Wheel of Fortune

World
The Lunar World into the Solar. (Threshold between Lunar and Solar Worlds.)

Wheel
The First Wheel or threshold of consciousness.

Beings
Angels, innerworld communicators, humans, ex-humans, lunar spirits or *daemones*. Also encompasses Elementals and other worlds such as faery realms.

Consciousness
Individual and collective thoughts and emotions; may be limited to one *persona* or include the fortunes of a family, group, race or nation. The interaction, in consciousness, between human beings and all other life forms on the planet.

Partner Trumps
Justice and Judgement (as higher harmonics).

Spheres and Planets
Spheres: The 7th and 8th Spheres, Victory and Glory.
Planets: Mercury and Venus.

Attributes

Fusion of thoughts and emotions: threshold of limiting consciousness between outer and inner energies of life. The wheel of a life cycle, the Seasons within humankind. Also the cycle of the Four Elements within the outer or sub-Lunar, and Lunar World. Conscious behind or within physical expression as form and interaction.

God and Goddess Forms

Fortuna (feminine image) Mercury and Venus. Minerva/Briggidda and the Flower Maiden in Celtic tradition. Relates to deities that cause changes in situations through their effect upon humankind (i.e. Mercury/Minerva as patrons of cultural development, Venus as goddess of love).

Key Phrases

Honour and victory/energy polarized as thoughts and feelings/change of fortune.

Merlin Texts

VM Merlin's journey around the Wheel of the Seasons.

Divinatory Meaning

A change of fortune (may be positive or negative). Often indicates, in association with other cards, how the individual's reaction will affect a cycle of events.

Related Number Cards

Sevens and Eights.
Sevens: Dishonesty, Ability, Humour, Attention.
Eights: Danger, Expediency, Excitement, Skill.

5
Justice

World
The Solar World. Reaches into the Stellar World. Threshold between Solar and Stellar consciousness.

Wheel
The Second Wheel; encompasses and incorporates the First Wheel, Fortune.

Beings
Archangels, angels; advanced innerworld communicators saints or masters.

Consciousness
Transpersonal, transhuman.

Partner Trumps
The Wheel of Fortune and Judgement (as spirals or harmonics).

Spheres and Planets
Spheres: The 4th and 5th, Mercy and Severity.
Planets: Mars and Jupiter.

Attributes
Catabolic and anabolic energies within the solar system. Creation and destruction and properties of spiritual

consciousness. The Goddess of Taking (Severity) and the God of Giving (Mercy). A perfect comprehension of the energies of adjustment.

God and Goddess Forms
Mars and Jupiter. The Morrigan (Severity) and the Daghda (Mercy or Goodness). All negative and positive polar partners and images.

Key Phrases
Adjustment/balance.

Merlin Texts
PVM The Goddess of the Land, balancing a forest in one hand and a city in the other; *VM* The king and queen hold a trial and judge Merlin.

Divinatory Meaning
Transpersonal energies of adjustment. Related to changes and interactions upon a spiritual level (just as The Wheel of Fortune relates to such changes upon a personal and collective level). May also relate to energies adjusting over long time cycles, similar to the Eastern concept of karma.

Justice always indicates essential adjustments that lead towards balance. It may be as direct as a court case or important decision, or it may be more profound in terms of deep adjustments in the individual.

Related Number Cards
Fours and Fives.
Fours: Truce, Generosity, Promise, Increase.
Fives: Loss, Retribution, Sorrow, Conflict.

6
Judgement

World
The Stellar World.

Wheel
The Third Wheel. Encompasses and incorporates Justice and Fortune.

Beings
Archangels, supernal entities.

Consciousness
Transhuman, transcendent.

Partner Trumps
Justice and The Wheel of Fortune as lower spirals or harmonics.

Spheres and Planets
Spheres: The 3rd and 2nd Spheres, Understanding and Wisdom.
Planets: Saturn and the Zodiac (or Neptune).

Attributes
Fusion of wisdom and understanding. The unknown limits and energies of the stellar originative universe. Absorption

and emission of consciousness/energy into and out of the origins of being. The cycle of creation and de-creation in its primal universal condition.

God and Goddess Forms
The Great Mother and the Star Father. Saturn and Neptune (Matrona and the Zodiac). The ultimate polarities of Being in the universe. Also images of space/time (3rd sphere) and energy (2nd sphere).

Key Phrases
Understanding/wisdom/ultimate judgement/total comprehension/perfection of energies.

Merlin Texts
PVM Vision of the goddess Ariadne who unravels the universe and summons the ancestral spirits.

Divinatory Meaning
May mean outwardly a matter of judgement in a situation, depending upon its position in the pattern of cards. Often indicates that a judgement must be made by the inquirer, often with profound or far-reaching effects. Also indicates collective or ancestral matters, such as national situations and seemingly unavoidable influences, but this level of meaning must be read only in association with all other factors.

Related Number Cards
Twos and Threes.
Twos: Doubt, Choice, Freedom, Change.
Threes: Suffering, Intention, Affection, Effort.

7
The Fool

World
Earth and all worlds.

Wheel
Travels through all Three Worlds, crossing all Three Wheels or thresholds. Relates initially, from an outer viewpoint, to The Wheel of Fortune.

Beings
Human.

Consciousness
Internalizing consciousness, particularly that of mind or intellect in quest of truth.

Partner Trumps
Polar partner: The Universe (World). Ultimate partner or reflection: The Innocent (Hierophant). Harmonic forms: The Magician, The Hanged Man and The Hermit (in ascending order).

Spheres and Planets
Spheres: 8th and 10th Spheres, Glory and Kingdom.
Planets: Mercury and the Earth.

Attributes
Relates to all other Trumps through cycles of experience. Is a master Trump, fully mobile and transformative. Relates specifically to internalizing or catabolic Trumps and energies. The original spirit within a human being. Intellect or mind becoming self-aware.

God and Goddess Forms
The man/woman, primal humanity The Child of the Great Mother. Mercury and Mother Earth.

Key Phrases
Innocence/questing mind/traveller/perfect folly.

Merlin Texts
H The young Merlin as innocent prophetic child, who ultimately utters the *Prophecies*; *VM* The Youth of Three Disguises (who later becomes The Hanged Man or Threefold Death).

Divinatory Meaning
Inspiration, spiritual impulse. May also indicate naïvety, or foolish idealism, in relationship to other defining cards. Often indicates moments or decision of great change and opportunity hidden within apparently difficult situations. The mysterious liberating factor that cuts across form, especially when The Hanged Man also appears in the pattern.

Related Number Cards
Tens (or Aces, see Figure 6) and Eights.
Tens: Disaster, Responsibility, Friendship, Opportunity.
Eights: Danger, Expediency, Excitement, Skill.

8
The Magician

World
The Lunar World.

Wheel
The First Wheel, Fortune.

Beings
Daemones, humans, ex-humans, ancestral spirits.

Consciousness
Human and collective or ancestral. May also relate to consciousness of other dimensions and beings, such as faery realms or elementals.

Partner Trumps
Polar partner: The Priestess. Harmonic forms: The Hanged Man, The Hermit. Relates also to the higher Trumps of Temperance and The Innocent (The Hierophant).

Spheres and Planets
Spheres: The 8th and 9th Spheres, Glory and Foundation.
Planets: Mercury or Hermes, and Luna.

Attributes

Hermes, the great initiator, through intellectual energies founded within controlled life forces. The organic growth of consciousness through individual effort. Educational traditions of magical arts and sciences. The questing intellect and collective sexual or foundational energies working together towards inner development and outer effects.

God and Goddess Forms

Luna and Hermes. May also be represented by certain primal deities concerned with magical arts; the instructing or shape-changing gods and goddesses who educate humanity.

Key Phrases

Honourable power/imagination for life/living magical arts/ glorious foundation of knowledge.

Merlin Texts

VM Taliesin (inspired by the goddess Minerva) expounds the nature and pattern of the universe.

Divinatory Meaning

Usually indicates matters of mental energy, life forces, and the creative use of the mind and imagination. Often shows, according to position, those aspects of the situation which would benefit from imaginative effort.

Related Number Cards

Nines and Eights.
Nines: Misfortune, Endurance, Fulfilment, Means.
Eights: Danger, Expediency, Excitement, Skill.

9
The Chariot

World
The Solar World.

Wheel
The Second Wheel, Justice.

Beings
Angels, innerworld masters and saints (ex-humans).

Consciousness
Transpersonal, catabolic or catalytic. May include aspects of personal intellect.

Partner Trumps
Polar partner: The Lovers (see also Figure 4).

Spheres and Planets
Spheres: The 8th and 6th Spheres, Glory and Beauty.
Planets: Mercury and Sol.

Attributes
Fusion of intellect or mind and spiritual awareness. The energies of thought and mental discipline as a vehicle for transcendent consciousness. Illumination leading to knowledge.

God and Goddess Forms
Hermes and Apollo: Minerva/Briggidda and Bel, the Lord of Light. Pagan goddesses of cultural development, patronesses of solar heroes. Inspirers and teachers of humankind on a transpersonal individual level that eventually benefits many.

Key Phrases
Glorious beauty/harmonious thought/knowledge in motion/higher awareness/inner teaching/vehicle of divine consciousness.

Merlin Texts
H, PVM, VM References to Minerva as patroness of knowledge and inspiration. Also references to transformative goddesses in general.

Divinatory Meaning
Higher knowledge, scientific inspiration and research. May also mean spiritual sciences and esoteric or Hermetic arts. Enlivening energy within the psyche of the inquirer or the situation, leading to a reasoned resolution inspired by insight.

Related Number Cards
Sixes and Eights.
Sixes: Transition, Balance, Joy, Benefit.
Eights: Danger, Expediency, Excitement, Skill.

10
The Guardian (The Devil)

World
The Solar World.

Wheel
The Second Wheel, Justice (connects Justice and the First Wheel, Fortune).

Beings
Angels, the solar archangel, ex-humans, innerworld masters or saints, inner adepts of magical arts.

Consciousness
Catabolic and transcendent.

Partner Trumps
Polar partner: The Empress. Higher harmonic: Death.

Spheres and Planets
Spheres: The 8th and 5th Spheres, Honour and Severity.
Planets: Mercury and Mars.

Attributes
Fusion of intellect or mind with solar energies of catabolism or purification. A guarding and inspiring power. Protector of

life forms (moving outwards) and destroyer of falsehood or illusion (moving inwards). Mysteries revealed through destruction of personal illusions.

God and Goddess Forms
Hermes and Mars. The ancient Lord of the Animals, protector and healer of lesser beings. Powers of breakdown embodied as male god forms.

Key Phrases
Honourable severity/purifying fire/Lord of the Animals/ Guardian of the Mysteries/Keeper of the Threshold/Initiator.

Merlin Texts
VM Merlin as Lord of the Animals, riding upon a stag.

Divinatory Meaning
Energies of purification, disillusion and rebalance. May indicate restriction for positive ends, as it often shows the inner or spiritual truth of a situation, according to position. Marks thresholds which it is dangerous to cross, or beyond which the individual overreaches his or her abilities. More rarely indicates magical or spiritual initiation within a given situation; will often provide the key to solutions for difficult problems or personal negative areas in life.

Related Number Cards
Eights and Fives.
Eights: Danger, Expediency, Excitement, Skill.
Fives: Loss, Retribution, Sorrow, Conflict.

11
The Blasted Tower

World
The Solar World.

Wheel
The Second Wheel, Justice.

Beings
Fiery or catabolic angels, the solar archangel. Innerworld beings concerned with purification and destruction.

Consciousness
Transpersonal.

Partner Trumps
Polar partner: Strength. Higher harmonics: Death, The Hanged Man.

Spheres and Planets
Spheres: The 5th and 6th Spheres, Severity and Beauty.
Planets: Mars and Sol.

Attributes
The blasting or breaking force inherent in the solar system and throughout the universe. The impersonal power of taking. Catabolism or catalysis causing change. Breakdown of form by force. The lightning flash.

God and Goddess Forms

Mars/Minerva and Apollo. Gods of sudden and inevitable force (the bolts of Apollo, the spear of Minerva). Images of divine retribution or purification. Represented in early Celtic legends by the destructive power of The Morrigan, goddess of battles.

Key Phrases

Beautiful severity/release from form/purification by fire/destroyer of corruption/spiritual lightning.

Merlin Texts

H A major motif in which king Vortigern builds a tower, undermined by the red and white dragons which are hidden in a cavern beneath its foundations. Leads to the *Prophecies* uttered by the youthful Merlin.

Divinatory Meaning

Breakdown and collapse of unhealthy, false or unnaturally rigid conditions. Destruction of illusions or delusions. May indicate material and physical breakdown or loss, depending upon position and other cards in the pattern. Sudden and often unexpected collapse or destruction within the query situation.

Related Number Cards

Fives and Sixes.
Fives: Loss, Retribution, Sorrow, Conflict.
Sixes: Transition, Balance, Joy, Benefit.

12
Death

World
The Stellar World.

Wheel
The Third Wheel, Judgement (links the Second Wheel, Justice, and Judgement).

Beings
Archangels, transhuman beings.

Consciousness
Transhuman, supernal. Corresponds to both superconsciousness and collective or ancestral consciousness on its most comprehensive level.

Partner Trumps
Polar partner: The Emperor (see also Figure 4).

Spheres and Planets
Spheres: The 3rd and 5th Spheres, Understanding and Severity.
Planets: Saturn and Mars.

Attributes
A feminine universal power of catabolic or inward-moving effect. Solar destructive and purifying energy fused with profound understanding. The ultimate dissolution of form and pattern, drawing energy back across the Abyss.

God and Goddess Forms
Mars/Minerva and the Great Mother. Death is a feminine figure, and all ancient goddesses of death, taking, dissolution and transhuman or total understanding partake of this image.

Key Phrases
A severe understanding/The Apple Woman/ultimate transformation/purifying understanding/The Sun at Midnight/return to the Mother/comprehensive change.

Merlin Texts
PVM Connections with the goddess Ariadne who unravels the universe; *VM* The Apple Woman who seeks to kill or madden Merlin (a motif from pagan Celtic mythology).

Divinatory Meaning
Initially means a change for the better. Implies that after dissolution and death comes new life. Often indicates total change and reorientation. On a higher level of understanding, frequently indicates changes which arise from deep inner or spiritual drives, causing outer form or patterns in the personal life to dissolve. May therefore indicate areas of personal tension and inner conflict that can be resolved only by true change.

Related Number Cards
Threes and Fives.
Threes: Suffering, Intention, Affection, Promise.
Fives: Loss, Retribution, Sorrow, Conflict.

13
The Hanged Man

World
The Stellar World (crossing the Abyss into the Solar World).

Wheel
The Third Wheel, Judgement, crossing the Second Wheel, Justice.

Beings
Saviours or redeemers, Sons of Light. Archangels, the solar archangel. Sacrificed kings and heroes. Innerworld communicators. The Order of Melchizadek or the Ancestral Kings.

Consciousness
Transpersonal.

Partner Trumps
Polar partner: Temperance. Relates also to The Fool as a master Trump.

Spheres and Planets
Spheres: The 3rd and 6th Spheres, Understanding and Beauty.
Planets: Saturn and Sol.

Attributes

The fusion of the Great Mother and the Son of Light. The paradox of sacrifice and the inversion of time, space and energy. Redemption and transformation through understanding. Inversion of all customary modes of awareness. Universal comprehension and knowledge centred upon one individual entity.

God and Goddess Forms

Saturn and Apollo. The Great Mother and her Son. All sacrificed gods, kings and heroes. Refers to Christ in orthodox Western religion, but encompasses a universal tradition embodied in various saviours.

Key Phrases

Beautiful understanding/universal harmony/sacrifice in full knowledge/keystone of the Arch of Heaven.

Merlin Texts

VM The Threefold Death.

Divinatory Meaning

Sacrifice of outer form or habits or situation for a non-personal or transpersonal end. Situations or instants of paradox, when a new level of understanding is gained. On a higher level, the card represents initiation into the Mysteries of Light. Often indicates outer situations of apparent loss or difficulty which lead in time to growth and increased awareness that transcends personality.

Related Number Cards

Threes and Sixes.
Threes: Suffering, Intention, Affection, Effort.
Sixes: Transition, Balance, Joy, Benefit.

14
The Hermit

World
The Stellar Originative World.

Wheel
Beyond the Third Wheel, Judgement.

Beings
Supernal consciousness withdrawing from individuation. Also relates to certain innerworld beings who choose remain as guides or inspirers of understanding, rather than cross into the void beyond being.

Consciousness
Transhuman universal.

Partner Trumps
Polar partner: The Innocent (Hierophant). Also relates to The Hanged Man, The Magician and The Fool as lower harmonics.

Spheres and Planets
Spheres: 1st and 3rd Spheres, Crown and Understanding.
Planets: Primum Mobile (Uranus in modern astrology) and Saturn.

Attributes

Withdrawal of super-consciousness inwards towards its ultimate source. The comprehension of transcendent truth.

God and Goddess Forms

Saturn and the Holy Spirit. Ideally represented by the Breath of Spirit within the Great Mother. All images that withdraw time and space: often mediated by ancient god forms such as the titans, but this is a property of human culture rather than an enduring set of god forms.

Key Phrases

Understanding truth/Inward comprehension/Light in darkness/Withdrawal into spirit.

Merlin Texts

VM Merlin withdraws as ancient wise man towards the close of the *Vita*: this withdrawal is related to stellar observation (the passage of time and supernal energies).

Divinatory Meaning

Often indicates that the inquirer must look within for proper answers to his or her question. Shows that understanding can be found through meditation, and that guidance is possible even in the darkest situation. May also indicate the close of a life cycle or period, and a withdrawal of energies accordingly, On an outer level, represents a period of self-examination and assessment. In the Merlin Tarot this Trump often appears in relationship to The Fool and/or The Hanged Man.

Related Number Cards

Threes and Aces.
Threes: Suffering, Intention, Affection, Effort.
Aces: Life, Light, Love and Law.

15
The Innocent
(The Hierophant)

World
The Stellar Originative World.

Wheel
Precedes The Third Wheel, Judgement.

Beings
Four Originative Powers or archangels. Divine universal being.

Consciousness
Originative being.

Partner Trumps
Polar partner: The Hermit. By reflection: The Universe or World and The Fool.

Spheres and Planets
Spheres: 1st and 2nd Spheres, Crown and Wisdom.
Planets: Primum Mobile (Uranus in modern astrology) and the Zodiac.

Attributes
The Crown of Wisdom. Perfect being emanating from an unknown source.

God and Goddess Forms
The Holy Spirit and the Zodiac or congregation of stars. The goddess Sophia or Holy Wisdom.

Key Phrases
Perfection/innocence/truth/the Original Name.

Merlin Texts
PVM Relationship to feminine deities such as the goddess Ariadne, and the Maiden who purifies the Land. No distinct reference.

Divinatory Meaning
Shows a spiritual originative power at work within any given situation or query. Indicates that a defined situation or pattern is enlivened by wisdom and truth; may be taken on a simple level as a positive indicator, dependent upon position and other cards. Often symbolizes powerful new beginnings in a life cycle or situation.

Related Number Cards
Aces and Twos.
Aces: Life, Light, Love and Law.
Twos: Doubt, Choice, Freedom, Change.

16
Temperance

World
The Stellar World, crossing the Abyss into the Solar World.

Wheel
The Third Wheel, Judgement, crossing the Second Wheel, Justice.

Beings
Archangels, saviours and Sons of Light. Special reference to the archangel or great consciousness of the Zodiac or the relationship between the sun and other stars. May also include certain transhuman modes of consciousness deriving from human foundations (as in traditions of men and women who have become 'archangelic').

Consciousness
Transpersonal, transhuman, universal.

Partner Trumps
Polar partner: The Hanged Man. (See also Figure 4.)

Spheres and Planets
Spheres: The 2nd and 6th Spheres, Wisdom and Beauty.
Planets: The Zodiac (or Neptune) and Apollo, Sol.

Attributes
A fusion of stellar and solar energies. Perfect balance and harmony, giving rise to immaculate transmutation and balance of force and form. Crosses the Abyss between universal originative energies and solar created patterns and life forms. Traditionally, the Path of the Redeemer or Son of Light, reaching into the created worlds.

God and Goddess Forms
The Zodiac and Sol. Neptune (as Lord of the Universal Ocean of Stars) and Apollo as the God of Light. Also indicates a transcendent non-sectarian image for the Saviour or Being of Light. The image is androgynous.

Key Phrases
Beautiful wisdom/perfection of power/universal transmutation/ The Bridge of Light.

Merlin Texts
VM Implied in higher stages of the Creation Vision.

Divinatory Meaning
May simply mean temperance or balance within the query situation; forces or consciousness that lead to a harmonious result. On a higher level may indicate grace or power from unknown sources or through previously untapped inner resources. Occasionally indicates a direct spiritual influence at work within the query.

Related Number Cards
Twos and Sixes.
Twos: Doubt, Choice, Freedom, Change.
Sixes: Transition, Balance, Joy, Benefit.

17
The Emperor

World
The Stellar World, crossing the Abyss into the Solar World, as does the partner Trump Death.

Wheel
The Third Wheel, Judgement (links Judgement and the Second Wheel, Justice).

Beings
Archangelic, transhuman.

Consciousness
Transhuman. Fusion of stellar and solar awareness.

Partner Trumps
Polar partner: Death. Lower harmonic: The Empress.

Spheres and Planets
Spheres: The 2nd and 4th Spheres, Wisdom and Mercy.
Planets: The Zodiac (Neptune in modem astrology) and Jupiter.

Attributes
The Great Giver. The explosion of energy and potential life across the Abyss into the created or Solar World. Corresponds to the Father God. Wisdom and Compassion.

God and Goddess Forms
The Zodiac or Father God, and Jupiter. The ancient Sky Father, the universal seed or potency of being which manifests as galaxies within the vessel of space and time.

Key Phrases
The Great Giver/the Compassionate Father/Merciful Wisdom.

Merlin Texts
PVM Vision of a white-haired man on a white horse, using a white wand to measure out dimensions of a river; *VM* Corresponds materially to the perfect king or emperor Rhydderch, the generous lord. Also inherent in the stellar creation described by Taliesin.

Divinatory Meaning
Illimitable creative power. May simply indicate a period or opportunity of great benefit, according to other cards and position. On a higher level, often shows opportunities for relationship between, and fusion of, inner and outer life and consciousness (crossing the Abyss in a state of wisdom). On an outer level, may also indicate fatherhood or involvement in situations where a fatherly or beneficial role is undertaken successfully.

Related Number Cards
Twos and Fours.
Twos: Doubt, Choice, Freedom, Change.
Fours: Truce, Generosity, Promise, Increase.

18
Strength

World
The Solar World.

Wheel
The Second Wheel, Justice.

Beings
Angels of building or blessing. The solar archangel. Inner-world beings concerned with positive or building energies and conditions.

Consciousness
Transpersonal.

Partner Trumps
Polar partner: The Blasted Tower. Higher harmonic: Temperance.

Spheres and Planets
Spheres: The 4th and 6th Spheres, Mercy and Beauty.
Planets: Jupiter and Sol.

Attributes
The anabolic or building power of the solar world. The giving and creative force that supports all form and life in the various worlds.

God and Goddess forms
Jupiter and Apollo. The blessing aspect of the Son of Light.

Key Phrases
Merciful beauty/harmonious compassion/giver of strength.

Merlin Texts
PVM Obscure reference to figure wrestling with a lion, not necessarily relevant; *VM* Indicated in the Creation Vision by profusion of creative force and beings.

Divinatory Meaning
A positive beneficial source of strength. May indicate power within a given situation, or may imply material benefit according to position and other cards. Often indicates creative or constructive possibilities within the query situation.

Related Number Cards
Fours and Sixes.
Fours: Truce, Generosity, Promise, Increase.
Sixes: Transition, Balance, Joy, Benefit.

19
The Empress

World
The Solar World.

Wheel
The Second Wheel, Justice (connects Justice and the First Wheel, Fortune).

Beings
Angels, the solar archangel. Innerworld beings and ex-humans.

Consciousness
Anabolic or building solar energies embodied within individual consciousness or collective consciousness.

Partner Trumps
Polar partner: The Guardian. Higher harmonic: The Emperor (see also Figure 4).

Spheres and Planets
Spheres: The 4th and 7th Spheres, Mercy and Victory.
Planets: Jupiter and Venus.

Attributes
Positive, giving, generous and blessing powers. Positive or healthy emotions within human consciousness. Life forces become attracted to one another and develop towards form.

God and Goddess Forms

Jupiter and Venus, the deities who confer blessings. The Lady of Flowers (or of Nature). The Goddess of Giving.

Key Phrases

Merciful victory/compassionate goddess/Lady of Flowers/ giver of life.

Merlin Texts

PVM A maiden vitalizes the land through mysterious forces; *VM* Merlin's wife Guendoloena.

Divinatory Meaning

Indicates a positive, giving state or condition. May relate to personal emotions or partners, or may symbolize a fruitful, creative or beneficial situation. Tends to indicate situations in which nurturing or cultivation are required to truly realize inherent potential, but this varies according to position and other cards in pattern.

Related Number Cards

Fours and Sevens.
Fours: Truce, Generosity, Promise, Increase.
Sevens: Dishonesty, Ability, Humour, Attention.

20
The Lovers

World
The Solar World.

Wheel
The Second Wheel, Justice.

Beings
Angels, the solar archangel. Ex-humans and transhuman teachers, innerworld masters or saints.

Consciousness
Spiritual energies reflecting as emotions. The creative or anabolic life force of the solar being.

Partner Trumps
The Chariot (see also Figure 4).

Spheres and Planets
Spheres: The 6th and 7th Spheres, Beauty and Victory.
Planets: Sol and Venus.

Attributes
Love as a spiritual power (rather than as a personal emotion). Emotions in their purest, most balanced mode or form. The perfect union of male and female energies within humanity,

either collectively or individually. Inner energies move towards life expression as polarized forms (male and female, positive and negative).

God and Goddess Forms
Apollo and Venus, the Lord and Lady of Light and Harmony. Also the mysterious Eros, who empowers the gods and goddesses.

Key Phrases
Harmony and victory/beautiful emotions/perfect partnership/mutual reflection of truth/spiritual love.

Merlin Texts
VM Relationship between Merlin and his wife Guendoloena. (This motif is, however, confused or rationalized in the *Vita* and is better represented by the Trump image.)

Divinatory Meaning
Love and relationships. Usually means positive, harmonious connections with other people (depending on position and other cards). May also mean a spiritual or transcendent power within the individual. Implies balance between male and female which may be outward- or inward-moving. Often represents inspired creativity, usually related to a lover or an idealized focus.

Related Number Cards
Sixes and Sevens.
Sixes: Transition, Balance, Joy, Benefit.
Sevens: Dishonesty, Ability, Humour, Attention.

21
The Priestess

World
The Lunar World (threshold to the Solar World).

Wheel
The First Wheel, Fortune.

Beings
Humans, ex-humans, certain transhumans or innerworld teachers; *daemones* and nature spirits, elementals.

Consciousness
Human emotional and imaginative consciousness.

Partner Trumps
Polar partner: The Magician. Higher harmonic Trumps: Strength, Temperance, The Innocent (Hierophant).

Spheres and Planets
Spheres: The 7th and 9th Spheres, Victory and Foundation.
Planets: Venus and Luna.

Attributes
Emotions and creative/reproductive energies. Tides of life power and swarms of life forms. Imagination forming or moulding reality in expression. A feminine anabolic and therapeutic consciousness/energy.

43

God and Goddess Forms

Venus and Luna, the goddesses of love and life, tides and feelings. All ancient goddesses relating to the positive emotions (attraction, love, sympathy, friendship). Goddesses or inner-world images connected to therapy, rebirth, transformation through the natural tides or cycles of the regenerative world (i.e. within the Wheel of Fortune). These goddess forms may also act as guides or initiators into the higher transpersonal consciousness of the Solar World.

Key Phrases

Victorious foundation of life/love as a power/the Mysteries of the Inner Fire/the Muse/Queen of the Fortunate Isles.

Merlin Texts

VM Vision of Morgen and her nine sisters ruling the Blessed Isle and curing the wounded King Arthur.

Divinatory Meaning

Relationship between emotions and foundational or sexual energies: often refers to mental and emotional health, matters of sexual attraction, reproduction, and creative work that employs the feelings. May also refer to insights into the inner Mysteries of life, either as maturity of emotions, or in the form of specific magical arts (such as meditation, visualization, prayer, or magical dance and music).

Related Number Cards

Sevens and Nines.
Sevens: Dishonesty, Ability, Humour, Attention.
Nines: Misfortune, Endurance, Fulfilment, Means.

22
The Universe
(The World)

World
The sub-Lunar or outer world, yet all worlds.

Wheel
The First Wheel, Fortune, but also all Three Wheels.

Beings
All living beings in the universe. Human beings on Earth.

Consciousness
Personal and collective. Also relates to the *Anima Mundi* or soul of the world in medieval metaphysics.

Partner Trumps
Polar partner: The Fool. Ultimate partner: The Hermit.
Harmonic forms: The Priestess and Temperance.

Spheres and Planets
Spheres: The 7th and 10th Spheres, Victory and Kingdom.
Planets: Venus and Earth.

Attributes
The consciousness of the world or universe. The Four Powers and Elements within all life forms. Encompasses universal being in an expressed individual image.

God and Goddess Forms

Venus or the Flower Maiden and the Earth gods and goddesses. Ultimately an androgynous being, often shown in alchemy and metaphysical imagery. By inversion, this is the divine androgyne, universal spirit inherent in matter.

Key Phrases

Victorious kingdom/perfection of Elements/universal being/divinity in matter/the universe within human awareness/manifest truth.

Merlin Texts

PVM Vision of the Goddess of the Land; *VM* Aspects of the Creation Vision relating to the Four Powers and Elements.

Divinatory Meaning

May simply mean worldly or material concerns, especially in the context of other cards. Also refers to balance of Elements or energies within the individual (according to position) and indicates outer or outcome parameters. Is also a direct indicator of where the greatest power may be found in any situation, according to the position of the card.

Related Number Cards

Tens (or Aces, see Figure 6) and Sevens.
Tens: Disaster, Responsibility, Friendship, Opportunity.
Sevens: Dishonesty, Ability, Humour, Attention.

2
The Number Cards

The Four Aces

The Ace of Birds

Element: Air; Direction: East; Suit: Swords or Arrows;
Power: Life; Keywords: Dawn, Spring, Beginning, Flight,
Birth, Morning

The Ace of Birds is the Eagle, ruling creature of the Element
of Air. Our image shows an Eagle bearing an Arrow to a Nest.
Eagles, hawks and other birds appear in certain Trumps, as
the Merlin Tarot is a tarot of living creatures. The presence of
the Ace of Birds causes powerful and disturbing new open-
ings, beginnings, changes. It is a card of great but unrealized
potential, of *originative* energy.

Depending upon other cards present in a pattern, the
Eagle can bring benefit or difficulty, life or death. Affiliation
with this creature and achieving a balanced relationship to its
power are difficult – air is a *difficult* Element. The difficulty
arises when the originative power manifests through expressive outer circumstances, and appears as a disruption. But

spiritual power will blow where it chooses, and we may not stand against it.

The power of Air, however, should not be considered as negative or suppressive. It is the inspiration of the spirit reaching the soul, it is the breath of life, of vitality, of being itself.

In most tarot decks the Ace of Air is shown as a Sword, first of the suit of Swords. Our Ace uses the Arrow, implement of flight, accuracy, and of penetrating to the heart or centre of its target.

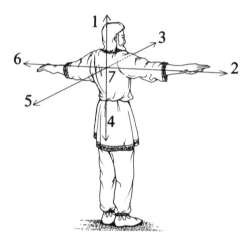

Figure 5: The Seven Directions

1 Above.
2 East (Before).
3 South (Right).
4 Below.
5 West (Behind).
6 North (Left).
7 Within.

The Ace of Serpents

Element: Fire; Direction: South; Suit: Rods or Wands;
Power: Light; Keywords: Summer, Noon

The Ace of Serpents is the Dragon, the creature of Fire and
Light. It is also represented by the Salamander, born of fire,
which appears, sometimes as a Serpent, in certain Trumps.

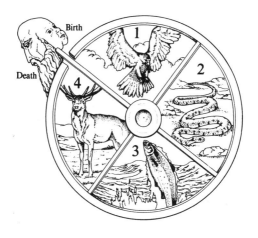

Figure 6: The Wheel of Life

1   East/Life/Air/Dawn/Spring/Birth/Sword/Birds.
2   South/Light/Fire/Noon/Summer/Adulthood/Rod/
    Serpents.
3   West/Love/Water/Sunset/Autumn/Maturity/Cup/Fishes.
4   North/Law/Earth/Night/Winter/Age/Shield/Beasts.

The Elemental powers and beings were sometimes described as four orders of supernatural being: Sylphs for Air, Salamanders for Fire, Undines for Water and Gnomes for Earth. Regrettably, this has been weakened by modern fantasy literature and cartoon images, but still forms the remnant of the old fairy Otherworld tradition.

The Dragon is the power of Light within the Earth, and it is the arousal of dragon power that causes Merlin, as a youth, to utter his prophecies. In one sense, the Dragon is the Element of Fire, the burning flame, while in a higher octave it is universal Light, the energy of being. The presence of the Dragon in a tarot pattern shows a balancing, affirmed power, an energy increasing in potency.

The implement of Fire is the Rod or Wand, or occasionally the Spear. In Christian religious dogma we find the archangel of the South, Michael, reputedly subduing the dragon with his spear. This is a corruption of an ancient god-vision, in which the god of light (Bel or Lugh in Celtic mythology) is associated with the dragon power.

Meditations upon the Dragon Ace bring arousal of our Inner Fire and Light, hence the use of the Rod for harmony balance and control.

The Ace of Fishes

Element: Water; Direction: West; Suit: Cups or Vessels; Power: Love; Keywords: Autumn, Evening

The Salmon is the creature of Water. In Celtic tradition the Salmon is the primal creature of deep wisdom, the great fish swimming in the waters of eternity. Although our modern minds tend to see fish as cold creatures, there is a long association of the fish with sexuality and fertility. The teeming shoals of fish in the mother ocean are manifestations of the Vessel of Love and Abundance.

The traditional implement of the West is the Cup, Cauldron or other Vessel. It signifies the Mystery of Love, of filling and emptying, of fruitfulness, of Autumn and evening. When the Ace of the West appears in a tarot pattern it reveals Love, either in a personal context or in a deeper spiritual sense, depending upon other cards present. It can indicate creativity, personal emotion, or the unbending strength and energy-source of the Vessel of the West.

The Direction of West is also associated with perfection and ideal spiritual vision, the Blessed Realm. The Vessel may also be the Grail, the Mystery of spiritual redemption and regeneration. There is a further association with physical birth and death, the vessel or gate passing from one world to another. The Ace of the West often enables human fertility and situations involving fruitful interaction.

The Ace of Beasts

Element: Earth; Direction: North; Suit: Shields or Mirrors; Power: Law; Keywords: Winter, Night

The Ace of Beasts is the Stag, king of the wildwood, lord of the four-footed creatures. The spiritual animal is strongly linked to Merlin as Lord of the Animals, referring to his period of madness in the forest, when he ran with the deer. This nature-aspect of the wild god also transforms into the goddess of the North, the Mother of the Land.

The traditional implement of Earth is the Shield or Mirror, and in our image the Stag's antlers frame a black

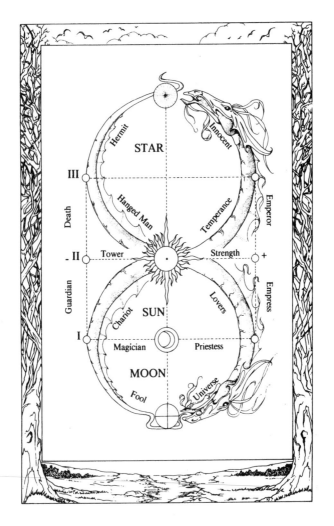

Figure 7: The Dragons, Worlds and Images

I. Lunar World (First Wheel).
II. Solar World (Second Wheel).
III. Stellar World (Third Wheel).

Mirror, which shows the fivefold pattern of the Merlin cosmology. In this pattern the Four Powers are unified by a central fifth. Within this we find a further pattern of four-in-one (or five), and so forth.

The presence of the Ace of Earth in a tarot pattern reveals manifest or expressed power, often concerned with outer or material circumstances. But its deep power is that of Law and Wisdom, the Mystery of Night and Winter. Thus it can indicate a force or restriction that leads to liberation, the Winter that precedes Spring, the wisdom of endings that bring beginnings. In the Celtic calendar night preceded day and Winter preceded Spring, so all cycles began not at dawn, but in the darkness.

The ultimate vision of the North is of the goddess Ariadne (or Arianrhod in Welsh tradition, Lady of the Silver Wheel). She is the Great Mother of the Stars, and her power is felt most strongly at night and in Winter.

The Four Twos

The Two of Birds

Doubt or Uncertainty
The Suit of Air, Direction East, is the power of Life, and is a suit of constant motion. The Two of Birds (Two of Swords in Renaissance tarot) is a vehicle of uncertainty, of rhythmic

polarity that may at time alter its pattern. It may return to its Ace, or it may act as a threshold into a Three or other number. Regarding a human situation, it often represents a pattern in which the outcome seems impossible to predetermine.

In the context of the cycle from North to East, night to dawn, the Two of Birds is the doubt that comes at the very brink of daybreak, at the point of stepping over. The fear inherent in the Air cards is a fear of the unknown, which blows through them all in various expressions.

If we use a keyword system for our initial experience of the numbers, we can relate them to the Elements and the Tree of Life. Thus, the Two of Birds is the Wisdom of Air: *Doubt! All life is uncertain; all is relative.* The power of Air is often one that breaks us down, leading to that terrible freedom when all known patterns, all secure situations, are blown away.

The Two of Serpents

Choice

With this Two we find will – it represents the polarities of either/or, positive/negative, yes/no. In Renaissance tarot this is the Two of Wands; it represents the two pillars of any choice, any balancing or polarizing situation. These should not be understood as antagonists, but as mutually connecting relative opposites, each defining and enabling the other. The choice is an act of will, of stepping through from one side to another, one world to another. Here the Ace, the primal Dragon of Fire and Light, empowering the Rod, radiates through first polarization. Gates and thresholds have not only a right and left, but an inside and outside. The inside is the Ace; the outside, the Three and the subsequent numbers.

In life situations this card shows there is a choice that can be made. In our progress around the cycle of Twos we are now coming towards fruition: change involving breakdown and renewal/doubt or uncertainty as to the direction of the newly inspired energies/choice is realized.

The keywords for this card are the Wisdom of Fire: *Choose well between right and left.* As for darkness and light, they depend upon one another. With the Two we cross from the primal light of the Dragon Ace of the South into the polarized light of the outer world, the Three. One light is darkness to the other, yet each is light, and could not shine without darkness.

The Two of Fishes

Freedom

This is the most kindly Two, if we may use such a term. In Renaissance tarot it is the Two of Cups. Cups or Fishes, Vessels or life forms, the Two of Water defines an easeful threshold. We swim through it comfortably toward the Three; it gives us a sense of release, of freedom. There is a further implication here of the emotions, associated with the Element of Water. In the Merlin Tarot, Beasts indicate the spirit and physical body, Birds the spirit and mind, Serpents or Dragons the Inner Fire of the spirit and soul, and Fishes the spirit and emotions. Law Life, Light and Love are all spiritual powers, but they flow through the body, mind, soul and emotions in human expression.

Our keyword for the Two of Fishes is the Wisdom of Love: *Freedom.* Love frees the spirit and soul, acting as a gateway through which we pass towards the number Three. It also frees the soul towards its spiritual origins, and with this directed love, we pass within to the Ace of Water, Love, perfect being.

The Two of Beasts

Change

In the North the Element of Earth is often felt to be the culmination or ending of any cycle, be it a day, a year or a lifetime. But the wisdom of the North is concerned with change arising out of darkness, night, stillness.

Figure 8: Circle, Spiral, Star: Three Worlds as human power centres.

The Two of Beasts (Two of Discs or Shields in Renaissance tarot) shows change arising out of the potential of Earth, the Direction of the North (see Figure 6). It can be a change of substantial power, and acts as a gate towards major transitions and movements of energy in any cycle, be it our own lives or that of any relative situation. It is the gate through which the power of the Ace passes towards outer expression: and through which our awareness passes as we move consciousness/energy towards the Ace in meditation and visualization.

The keyword for the Two of Beasts is the Wisdom of Earth: *All things change.* Even within the apparent solidity of matter is the energy of perpetual change.

The Four Threes

A triple pattern was frequently found in Celtic tradition as Three was considered a number of power. It derives from an ancient triple world view, and is retained in the Merlin Tarot and in Northern and Western myth and esoteric traditions as the Three Worlds (see Figure 1, p.ix).

Threes correspond to the Triads or balanced (sealed or completed) power patterns of the Tree of Life (see Figures 2 and 11, pp.xi and 69). They also reveal the Three Worlds of Star, Sun and Moon.

The triple pattern was frequently at the foundation of ancient ritual, myth and magic. Even using the word 'foundation' leads us to the 9th Sphere of the Tree of Life (3+3+3), which is the pivot of the Lunar World, the Moon, realm of the Ninefold or Triple Goddess.

The Three of Birds

Suffering

Air cards are frequently 'difficult'; the power of Air is that of changing winds, wild inspiration, tumult. The energies of the Air suit are those of ecstasy and agony. We frequently misunderstand that spirit (the breath of being) brings drastic change, and if we resist this spiritual transformation, we suffer. The suffering arises from unresolved forces within ourselves.

The Three of Birds is the Understanding of Air, *the Suffering of the Mother*. It has resonances of giving birth, for from Two to Three is the movement of birth, but the birth and suffering are often upon the level of the spirit, reaching into the mind and soul. The higher numbers tend towards physical manifestation, while the lower numbers tend towards inner and metaphysical dimensions, though we should not take this idea too literally.

The ancient augury pattern for this power shows when a pair of mating birds or a flock of birds tussle with another type of bird in the air. Watching the movement of birds in flight gives deep insights into the Air suit. The collective wheeling of large flocks, for example, still a mystery to modern science, reveals the power of the Ten, where many together suddenly break into ones, then re-form as one unit made of many.

The Three of Serpents

Intention

Serpents/Dragons are creatures of Fire in the South. In geomantic or planetary terms, they embody the fire within the Earth, the light of the land. In human terms, they are the

Inner Fire and light, the spiritual power inherent within our bodies. There is an unfortunate tendency for modern meditators to separate the so-called 'higher powers' from the body, but in the primal traditions there is no such separation. Hence the Serpent or Dragon that is a creature of Fire and Light.

The Suit of Serpents (Wands) is concerned with will and increasing energy. The keywords for the Three are *The Serpents of Understanding* or *Understanding Fire*. Here the uncertainty of the Two, in which polarities were constantly alternating, is left behind. Through an intentional act of understanding, seeking to cross, seeking comprehension, the Two becomes Three. The converse direction is where we choose to leave all intent and known patterns behind, and (intentionally) enter the Two, the state of uncertainty that marks the threshold towards the Ace, the primal Dragon of Fire and Light.

Three is the Mother number, and Six (3+3 or 3×2) is the number of the Sun and the Child of Light. Nine (3+3+3 or 3×3) is the number of the Moon, and the incarnation of spirit into matter. The cycle of Threes resonates with the Trump of The Star, the cycle of Sixes resonates with the Trump of The Sun, and the cycle of Nines with the Trump of The Moon. There is a wealth of meditational material in these connections.

The Three of Fishes

Affection

Fishes, the suit of the West, of Water, of Love as a spiritual power, are frequently cards of the emotions. They show the transition and relationship between our feelings and the deeper spiritual powers flowing from the Ace (Cup or Vessel) that is the universal power of Love. As already mentioned, while modern people tend to think of the fish as a cold creature, its primal significance is quite different. The fish in water was a powerful sexual fertility symbol, and in Celtic tradition the creature of wisdom was the Salmon.

In the Ace of Fishes we see the Salmon leaping upstream, and the Cup or Vessel. In the Two we see liberty or freedom of movement through Love flowing from the Ace. In the Three we find the Understanding of Water. The affection in our keyword is not a weak or temporary emotion, but that steady and constant timeless affection that is more powerful than personal emotion or romantic love that seeks gratification. It is that deep affection seen between mother and child, an unconditional state of love. In another expression, which works through time, it is that deep affection that grows between friends or partners who have spent time together and shared many experiences.

The Three of Beasts

Effort

The number Three and the Element of Earth give rise to the Three of Beasts or Shields, a card in which the changeability of the Two is stabilized and temporarily paused. The keyword is the Understanding of Earth: *Expressive Comprehension, Effort.* The effort is initially made to move beyond the choice of the Two, but soon becomes the effort of unlocking the Three towards the Four. Threes in the North are triads of power working through manifest patterns; in life situations they show right effort towards a graceful or wise end.

The Four Fours

The Four of Birds

Truce

The Four of Air (Birds or Swords) mitigates the turbulence and cutting power of the Ace. In other words, it takes the *suffering* of the Three, and reduces it *mercifully*. The keywords are *Merciful Air* or *Spirit of Compassion*.

In societies where close-contact manual weapons were commonplace, we find a curious archaic form of warfare in which the combatants seldom sought to wipe each other out. The rules, widespread in ancestral cultures, by which warlike situations were resolved without slaughter, were those of Truce and Championship.

Modern 'truces' tend to be mere political manipulative scenarios, our inheritance from the Roman-style civilization in which outward legalizing, hiding inward martial force, replaced nurturing social concepts. A military truce, once a time for wise consultation or sowing of crops, or rest before single combat, has become a veil over covert aggression.

The Four of Birds has many implications beyond outer conflict and truce, of course. It represents a *breathing-space* (Air in the Four Elements), a giving-pause during which the turbulent, irresistible force of the Ace is balanced briefly by the number Four. The next major location or state of balance is the Six of Birds. As a gate the Four of Air offers each of the Four Directions, and a truce in which to survey the territory and make a further decision.

In life situations this is an important card for awareness of potentials, or rhythm. If we are not able to perceive it, it can slip by too easily and suddenly turn into the Five.

Figure 9. The Expansion of Numbers

The Four of Serpents

Generosity

The Four of Fire (Serpents or Rods) is a card of giving without cost. It is that generosity which asks no return, and when
we encounter it in life it is the building, giving power that
aids us in any situation or pattern. It works on a physical level
as the Four Elements building, balancing and regenerating
the forces within us, and on a personal or emotional and
mental level as the vast potential of power into which we may
tap if we truly choose to do so.

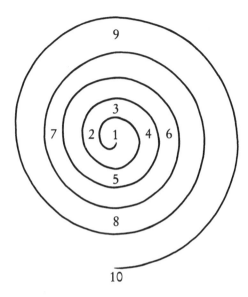

Figure 10: The Rotation of Numbers

Its keywords are *Fire of Compassion* or *Merciful Dragon*. It represents that potential of giving that comes from a total selflessness, an established energy attuned to the universal power of Mercy, the giving gods and goddesses.

It is that merciful power to which people pray, through the images of their various religions, when they seek intervention and kindliness from fate. But the secret of the Four of Fire is that it has to flow *through us* and *out of us*.

The Four of Fishes

Promise

The Four of Water (Cups or Vessels) is a card of what are sometimes called 'higher emotions', though in primal wisdom traditions the ideas of 'higher' and 'lower' do not involve antagonism or dualism. Its keywords are *Promise of Mercy* or *Creative Compassion*. As a double gate, the Four of Water (West, evening, fruitfulness, giving and receiving) is the expansion, the flooding tide, of the affection that we encountered flowing through the Three.

Its promise is that of spiritual mercy, the promise of a giving power that will compassionately respond to our needs. This is a subtle idea, for *needs* and *wants* are often confused in the Fours, Sevens and Nines. If what we need in a life situation is a total undercutting, breakdown and devastating change, then that is what eventually comes to pass, but beyond it is the Promise of Mercy. Many compassionate spiritual abilities are realized through the Four of Water: healing; empathy; transpersonal love; forgiveness and taking away, washing or dissolution of soul-burdens.

The Four of Beasts

Increase

The Four of Earth (Beasts or Shields) is a card of growth; its keywords are *Merciful Earth*. It is the further gate or threshold after the effort of the Three. Four Beasts form the first true increase of a herd, for two pairs may breed on, generating offspring in polarized patterns with many potentials. The 4th Sphere upon the Tree of Life is Mercy, the planet is Jupiter, and the god and goddess forms are all those of *giving*. The nature of an Ace or primal power will flow through the

Four and attune it, but as a double gate (2+2), Four is the greatest giving power that we may experience. It flows outwards, towards or into increasing manifestation.

In human circumstances the Four of Beasts enables increase in any existing situation; it gives power to it and expands it. Keywords for all the Fours are *expansion* or *opening*, while for the Fives they are *contraction* or *closing*. The hinge between Four and Five is the number-pattern of our current situation in Western technological society. We have taken and received so much, generated so many greedy potentials and situations out of the merciful Earth, that we can only be balanced by the vigorous taking force of the Fives.

The Four Fives

The Five of Birds

Loss
The Five of Air (Birds or Swords/Arrows) is a card of *movement*. The power of Air becoming Five blows patterns and situations away. Its keywords are *The Taking Wind* or *The Birds of Loss*.

As an Air card, the Five of Birds is often related to loss or abandonment in early phases of a situation, but it may also appear as a power in collapsing patterns. The conflict of the Five of Beasts can lead to the loss of the Five of Birds. Separation and breaking up of established patterns (Earth) bring a bleak beginning (Air). The Five of Birds is a number in which we are not even aware of the beginning, only that known patterns or situations (Fours) have been spirited away by the Taking Wind.

The Five of Serpents

Retribution

The Five of Fire (Serpents or Rods) is an active power of rebalance; it counteracts the increase of the Four. This is generated by the Aces of Life and Light flowing into the form of Five, in which the double gate is sealed by a fiery power, which conles any further expansion. The keywords here are the *Purifying Fire* or *The Flaming Pentagram*. Any entity or energy seeking to pass through the Five is rebalanced by its conling flame.

Retribution is a complex idea, too often used as propaganda. In the purest sense of the word (from the Latin), it means *assigning back* or paying back tribute – retribution is the balancing return for either good or evil. Popularly, we colour it with notions of retribution for evil or for infringement of authoritarian rules, but this is the most superficial and propagandist level of the power of the Five of Fire. Inwardly it involves an act of will (Fire cards frequently define will and creative forces of consciousness): we *choose* to invoke the power of Fire in the number Five, to seek rebalance. In this sense retribution has a therapeutic connection, as the cauterizing fire, the surgical laser, the healthy Inner Fire that leads to vitality and purification of the blood.

The Five of Fishes

Sorrow

The Five of Water (Fishes, Cups or Vessels) ends the promise of the Four. It is the Fifth Vessel that pours out its contents, emptying the accumulated flow of energy from the Ace of Love. The Direction of West is frequently associated with longing, sorrow, and that mysterious grief for our lost paradise or primal world. The card may represent personal sorrow in a direct situation, but more frequently defines the deep sorrow of the soul.

Keywords here are *Flowing Away* or *Ebb-tide*. The Five Fishes are the shoal of promises that vanishes into the Ocean, the paradise over the horizon. These are not vague romantic longings, but true representations of our loss, our separation of the true perfect world from the corrupted world that we have imaged and built through our increasing power of materialization.

The Five of Beasts

Conflict

The Five of Earth (Beasts or Shields) shows tension or conflict. It marks the maximum increase of the Four to a condition in which a balancing force of decrease must appear. The conflict can be between opposing forces or interests, but they have grown out of the Four. Five is the closing of the gate of Four. The keywords are *Earth's Severity* or *The Breaking Earth*. Any gardener knows that the Earth gives and takes equally: to have vigorous growth there must be a cycle of decay. This applies to human life just as it applies to the land and the planet.

The conflict of the Five of Earth is that of adjustment of pattern, of energies and entities seeking the balance of a new cycle or further pattern. To find this the old pattern must first be broken down. It can revert to Four or move on to Six.

As we are working with Five, the power of taking, this is the place to remind ourselves that though a Four can flow directly to Six or Seven in terms of beneficial expression, its balancing power may be realized in the Nines or Tens of Air, powers of extreme breakdown. Five is the number of humanity, and if we address its power within ourselves, upon its own level or state of consciousness, there will be less outer disaster or severe limitation in our expressed lives.

The Four Sixes

The Six of Birds

Transition

The Six of Air (Birds, Swords, Arrows) is a card that tends to modify the turbulent, changeable effect of the Ace of Air. Six is a harmonizing number, and the Six of Birds shows movement from one state to another, a balanced transition. There is also a sense of movement towards sanctuary, safety or settlement in the Six of Air.

Keywords for this card might be *Beautiful Flight* or *Harmony of Birds*. This second key phrase brings us to the musical attributes of the number Six. A sequence of birdsong is an air transition, sound as defined shape. Music consists of shapes within shapes in Elemental cycles that resonate within our consciousness, and even into our physical substance. The Six of Air might, in a rather restricted classical music scenario, be interpreted as a fugue and variation pattern. In fundamental tones or empowered musical calls, it is the overtone or harmonic sequence inherent in any emission of sound. The Six of Air is where 'chaos' and 'order' are found inherent within in one another; harmonized flows of shape, energy and music, within the holism of the worlds.

The Six of Serpents

Balance

The Six of Fire (Serpents or Rods) is a number of poise, of balance. The keywords might be *Illuminating Beauty* or *Perfected Fire*. As Serpents and Rods are vehicles of the true will or spiritual intent, the Six embodies this will and its Fire energies in a condition of balanced power. This is not resting or static, but energizing and active to such an extent that is perfectly poised over the centre of being. One key model here is that of the spinning-top or gyroscope. We might visualize the Six as a wheel with six spokes or as a resonating sphere of power in perfect alignment.

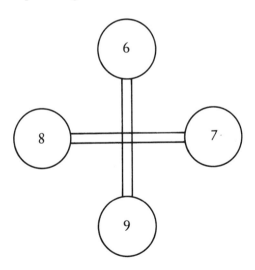

Figure 11: The Triads of Numbers

The solar power is equally creative and destructive. Balance (the Six of Fire) is the pattern of the solar system, the planets, the orbits, the relationships. In a mystical sense, it is the harmonizing and redeeming will of the Son or Daughter of Light, enabling life for all beings within the holism of the Solar World.

The Six of Fishes

Joy

The Six of Water (Cups, Vessels, Fishes) is a card of flow, of giving, of receiving. The joy that it contains is a selfless joy, often found as the ecstasy of spiritual enlightenment. As a Water power, it harmonizes the flow of the Ace from the West, transforming its power of Love into beauty and sharing. The keywords here are *Singing Harmony* and *Sea of Beauty*.

The joy of the Six of Water is a sharing joy, it is that joy of union that comes with sexual ecstasy and mystical ecstasy. The two joys have been wrongly separated due to orthodox religious conditioning in the West, but they are the same joy. All spiritual powers are sexual, all sexual powers are spiritual.

In a creative sense, it is the joy of creation, in which the giving power, the flow of the Ace, is shaped and harmonized by the Six into a beautiful pattern, to be given freely to others, that they might see the inherent beauty of it. In a sexual sense, it is that joy of souls mingling, rather than isolated gratification or selfish sex, that joy that can lead to spiritual realization, or may lead to the incarnation of a joyful soul.

The Six of Fishes holds many insights into the harmony of spiritual sex and the calling or singing in of souls into the vessel that leads, through the Nines, towards physical birth.

The Six of Beasts

Benefit
The Six of Earth (Beasts or Shields) is a beneficial power. Its keywords are *Harmony of Earth* or *Beautiful Land*. The power of Six is solar and centralizing, and often acts as a healing and redemptive force. As the Ace of Earth resonates through the number Six, it confers a beautifying and blessing power upon situations, entities and energies.

Six may also be understood as 3+3, the Hexagram of Harmony. In Earth the Three embodies effort, and a double Three shows this effort reflected. The Hexagram shows the fusion of Worlds: the Stellar and Lunar Worlds as triads, or triangular poised patterns, merge as the Solar World. Thus effort brings benefit in our outer worlds – but only if the inner dimensions of energy are harmonized.

The Four Sevens

The Seven of Birds

Dishonesty
The Seven of Air (Birds, Swords, Arrows, Direction East) is often a card of self-deceit. The mind talks itself out of truth, and the turbulent power of Air disrupts the emotions. In broader terms, it is a card of complex movement. It can, therefore, indicate intentional dishonesty, in which the thought and will generate a false situation or false emotions.

Keywords here are *Original Victory* and *Dawn of Feeling*. These crucial modes of *beginning*, the Ace of Air flowing through into the number Seven, often appear as impulsive patterns of emotion. These are dishonest not through will or

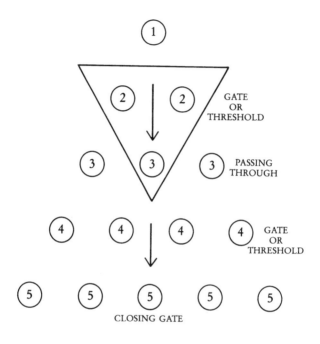

Figure 12: The Polarity Thresholds

conscious choice, but because they are followed willy-nilly without any reflection or attention (Seven of Earth) to bring them into balance.

The dishonesty of the Seven of Air is in many ways the 'opposite-opposite' of the Seven of Earth. This is shown upon the Wheel of Life, for after the grace of the Seven of Earth comes the potential dishonesty (temptation) of the Seven of Air. We must always remember that we tempt ourselves – no outside agency can ever do so – and so we are always responsible both for our own temptations and our response to them. The Sevens are cards of the feelings, the emotions, of power energies that tend to reflect themselves in increasingly glamorized or potentially deluding patterns. Yet the Elemental Cycle and the Directions of the Four Sevens hold perfect balance and all the necessary powers for our return to grace.

The Seven of Serpents

Ability
The Seven of Fire (Rods or Serpents, Direction South) reveals the increasing manipulating or organizing power of will. Whereas in the Six this power was spiritual, creative will or intent, it now moves forward to fuse the intent and the feelings. The ability is not a conditioned or trained ability, but that natural feeling for any act or activity that brings it to a victorious conclusion. It is the light of ability in the South reflected to and from the mirror of attention in the North.

Keywords here are *Victorious Fire* or *Triumph of Illumination*. The Seven Wands or Rods are the markers of Sacred Space upon a ground-plan, the layout of the sacred land or geomantic zone. They represent the ability of human consciousness to define, perceive and relate to Elemental, planetary and stellar forces.

Other keywords for this card are *Fiery Serpent* or *Loving Dragon*. This aspect of the Seven of Fire refers to energies within ourselves and within the sacred land: the human emotions and their equivalent geomantic forces, those of hidden fire or energy within the land. There is, again, a powerful sexual movement to the Seven of Fire; it can show sexual ability, which is balance and loving relationships of the Inner Fire. This same Fire flows through the land (sometimes called the Green Fire, though this is merely a convenient symbol as the colours may vary from place to place and time to time) and is the equivalent of sexual energy aroused, related, balanced and made fruitful.

The Seven of Fishes

Humour

The Seven of Water (Cups, Fishes, Direction West) reveals the Ace of Love flowing through our feelings. It is that sense of humour which is spontaneous and deep, bringing clear laughter, free of personality or pose. Keywords here are *Star of Laughter* or *Triumph of Feeling*. Laughter is a powerful spiritual declaration – when we truly laugh, we allow the inner Love to manifest directly through our body, through our voice. Real laughter is always spontaneous, surprising, never planned.

Humour is a hallmark of a clear soul (as the Seven is clear in the sense of being sustained and washed by the Element of Water). The ability to bring humour into people's lives is a spiritual gift. By this we should not accept or devise vicious comedy or intellectually contrived wit, for these are lesser aspects of true humour, comprised of mixed numbers or Elements, which are often in imbalance when themes of cruelty are present.

The Seven of Water is also the sexual laughter that rises unbidden in ecstasy: the Seven Cups or swimming Fishes are the union of male and female, and the climax of energies that leads to further life. The union may be understood as two intersecting triangles (Six) with a perfect point or seed of

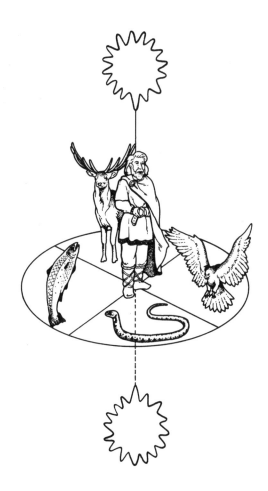

Figure 13: The Seven Creatures and Seven Directions

fusion and origination in the centre (Seven). The Seven, however, does not ensure fertility, but forms the energetic emotional sexual conditions in which a soul may be attached to parents. The further stages towards physical birth are in the Eights and Nines.

There is sometimes a sense of self-delusion to the Seven of Water, often where romantic choices and images are taken too seriously, or accepted without any proper attention to their effect. The Seven of Fishes or Cups is, in this sense, rising towards or filling with the unstable dishonesty of the Seven of Swords or Birds. The humorous heart, however, will always clarify delusions, for a balanced emotional pattern is one in which we cannot take ourselves seriously.

The Seven of Beasts

Attention

The Seven of Earth (Beasts, Shields or Mirrors, Direction North) embodies the Ace crossing from the harmonized energies of the Six and expanding towards expression or manifestation. The Seven of Beasts or Shields has moved beyond the triple gate of Six, and focuses its energies upon *formative victory*. This card has the power of building, of defining, of structuring, in readiness and preparation for a further step or steps towards Ten. Its keywords might be *Attending the Earth* or *Venus Reflecting*.

Venus is also the morning and evening star, the definer of the thresholds crossed between night and day. Attention to the rising and setting of Venus over the horizon, and to the rising and setting of her powers within ourselves, brings a pattern, a rhythm. The Seven of Earth is concerned with patterning the flowing energies of the emotions and sexuality, the attractive forces of nature. By giving our attention to these forces consciously, rather than being unconsciously dominated by habits moulded from these forces (or conditioned into us by circumstances), we find the *Victory of Earth*, which is, in its highest spiritual form, Grace.

The Seven of Earth is that pattern of Sacred Space enlivened when we face North. Traditionally, the Shields, Mirrors, Crystals or Lenses of Earth are located in each direction: Above is the Mirror of Night; Below is the Mirror of the Underworld. Before us in the North is the Mirror of Winter and Earth, Behind us is the Mirror of Summer and Fire. To our Right is the Mirror of Spring and Air, to our left is the Mirror of Autumn and Water. Within is the Mirror of Truth, Being, the Ace of Law and Liberty.

The Four Eights

The Seven of Birds

Danger

The Eight of Air (Birds, Swords, Direction East) is a card of uncertainty and potential destructive or disruptive energy. It represents that danger that may be passed through, but has to be addressed, either in potential or in reality, come what may. As an Air card the Eight opens the Four Gates to the Four Winds, and the blast of their coming together disrupts our accustomed patterns.

In the Apocalypse of Merlin, found in the *Prophecies*, Ariadne, the Weaver Goddess, unravels the solar system, causing the ordered cycle of the planets and Zodiac Signs to disintegrate. She then withdraws her presence into the originative crack or source from which the worlds were emitted, and the Four Winds come together with a blast that is heard by the distant stars. This is the cosmological vision of the Eight of Air, in the Stellar and Solar Worlds.

In the Solar and Lunar Worlds, however, its effects are modified by relative patterns. That which is dangerous for one individual or group is safe for another. Skill plays a great part in the relative danger of any situation.

Keywords are *Encircling Wind, Ceaseless Change, Restless Motion*. The danger can equally come from within as from without. It is the danger that comes from uncentred restlessness, from seeking ceaseless change for no reason. It can, under extreme circumstances, break out as violence in the individual or group, creating a danger to others. As Air cards are concerned with the mind and mental activity, the Eight of Birds may also be a card of mental disturbance, imbalance and confusion.

The Eight of Serpents

Expediency

The Eight of Fire (Rods or Serpents, Direction South) is the fourfold pattern of Twos, the pillars of the Four Gates. Because the pillars represent polarity, the Eight is a card of constant interchange of energies. It moves with great rapidity, and will take whatever action is necessary to rebalance and enable the intent of the mind. Expediency means taking whatever action is right at any moment; its negative possibilities spill over into dishonesty, dishonour and politics.

Keywords for this card are *Creating Possibilities, Glory of Wands, Wisdom of Serpents*. Wisdom (Two) is a higher octave of Glory (Eight), just as Understanding (Three) is a higher octave of Victory (Seven). But while Wisdom and Understanding tend to be universal polarities, the Star Father and the Great Mother, Victory and Honour are teeming with sexually polarized interchanging beings. These are the swarms of potential life often described in creation myth, in esoteric teachings and mystical cosmology.

The Eight of Fire is a card of *interchange*: the danger of the winds of Air causes balancing, expedient action to be taken. Fire cards, Serpents, Rods, are all concerned with will and intent. Again we have the keyword for the 8th Sphere, Honour or Glory, to remind us that the intent must be unselfish for the power of the Eight to flow fully.

The Eight Rods of this card are the four fingers of two hands, or the upper and lower arms and legs. There is an eightfold pattern in the manipulative extending bones of the human skeleton, which manifests the universal pattern and elemental being in human form.

The Eight of Fishes

Excitement

The Eight of Water (Cups, Fishes, Direction West) is a power of fluid motion. Keywords here are *Forming Glory* or *Cascade of Energy, The Swimming Shoal*. This last phrase uses the image of a seething shoal of fish, endlessly turning and forming patterns out of their living movement and relative positions, a whole entity as a shoal, yet many excited individuals.

The Element of Water flows through the gates and forms complex interacting patterns. In fluids these flow-patterns are of infinite variety, and form part of the 'new' mathematics and physics that uses computer generated models and fractal systems. The fluid dynamic patterns are those of the Elements: each Element has within it relative patterns of all four.

The excitement of the Eight of Water may be mental, emotional or sexual, or an interplay of all three. The Eight (thought, communication) causes the mind to seethe with possibility, with anticipation, to be restless and full of expectation. It often involves thought leaping ahead of itself, looking forward to a specific event, manifestation or meeting.

As Eights tend to be cards of mental activity and communication, they often reveal our inner responses to outer situations. The Eight of Water, being the infinite flow of potentials, is also a card of reproduction, though not always in the physical, sexual sense. It is involved with the thought processes of artistic creation, the excitement of forming a work, an image, a project of any sort. It is also a card of cooperation, of many potentials flowing together, the excitement of working with and relating to others.

The Eight of Beasts

Skill

The Eight of Earth (Shields, Direction North) embodies the power of the Ace through mind working with substance. Keywords are *Glorious Expression* or *Honourable Mind, Earth Skills* or simply *Quicksilver*. Eight is 4×2, or 2+2+2+2. Thus, it represents the Four Gates of the Quarters, and offers the definitions or skill to work with their energies and forms.

There is a further implication in the Eight of Earth, for it reveals manipulative skill. This honourable skill is that of the fingers working upon substance. Its converse, of course, is dishonourable manipulation for selfish ends.

In Greek myth Mercury (the 8th Sphere) was the inventor of the lyre, a stringed instrument with cosmological significance. While the human digits are ten, the fingers are eight in number. Our thumbs are the expressive digits of Earth, making the Right and Left Pillars of the Kingdom or 10th Sphere, and without them the fingers cannot work. But the eight fingers are the fast-moving, skilful manipulators of substance, of form, of inventive techniques and communicative devices. The eight fingers are also the Eight Rods or Serpents in the Eight of Fire, Fire and Earth being complementary opposites or polar reflections of one another.

The Four Nines

The Nine of Birds

Misfortune

The Nine of Air (Birds, Swords or Arrows, Direction East) is a power of taking or breaking. The Eight, Nine and Ten of Air are difficult and unavoidable powers; they may be balanced, but not cheated or escaped. As Air approaches outer expression, so it becomes more dangerous, complex and cutting or blasting.

The Nine of Air is 3×3 or 3+3+3, the Mother of Mothers, with keywords such as *Bringer of the Whirlwind, Birth of Sorrow*. This card is frequently associated with pain, with birth pangs and death pangs. The pain may be physical, mental, emotional or spiritual. Spiritual pain is the Sorrowing Mother of all being (the 3rd Sphere), physical pain is the birth or death of any life-phase within our organism. This too, is a type of motherhood, whether you are male or female. Air cards are often concerned with therapy and imbalance, and the greater numbers can indicate occurrences or periods of physical illness as well as mental and emotional disturbance.

As Air is such a mobile Element, there is often surprise or suddenness associated with its greater numbers. This is the storm that breaks unexpectedly, the whirlwind that rises from the calm sea, the sudden accident. Its misfortune is associated with cutting and separation, loss and diminishment.

One important key to this card is that it is the power of separation that brings beginnings. But within its storm, at the moment of flight or loss, we cannot perceive what or where or who the beginning might be.

The other Nines – the endurance of Serpents, the fulfilment of Fishes and the means of Beasts – help us, however, to contemplate and understand this power. The misfortune of the East is balanced by, or takes from, the fulfilment of the West, flowing between means in the North and endurance in the South (see Figure 14).

The Nine of Serpents

Endurance

The Nine of Fire (Serpents or Wands, Direction South) is the firmly founded will and strong intent. Its endurance is that of the Three of Fire (intention), tripled into expression and manifestation. Keywords here are *Enduring Fire* or *Immutable Foundation*.

The Nine embodies the Fire and Light power emerging in its last step towards manifestation. It is the connecting force, the intent to remain in a structure, a shape, a pattern. In human terms it is endurance of will, in which we hold ourselves together through all misfortunes. There is a further aspect of imagination in the Nine of Fire, for it represents the will creating images in the inner light, the imaginative pool out of which dreams are made substantial and expressed as outer patterns. The technique of empowered and guided visualization is a perfect example of the Nine of Fire: the will generates and reinforces images, while the images give us further power to perfect our will. But this is not a closed system or dogmatic in any way.

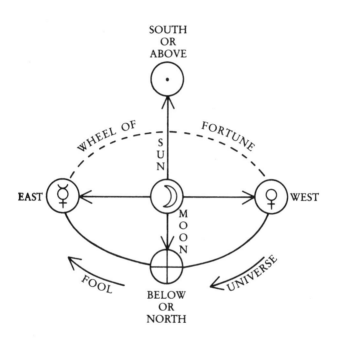

Figure 14: The Ninefold Power Pattern

We must be wary of confusing the endurance of the Nine with obstinacy or rigidity. The triple Three is a pattern of foundation, but it does not last forever. Its immutability is often that of regeneration, for any of its three Threes can regenerate a further cycle, just any two Threes or all three Threes will work towards an end, towards Ten in one direction or One in another.

There is sometimes a sense of burden and weight with the Nine of Fire, knowing that the intent will carry us through a difficult situation and imagining the potentially good outcome. By such imagination, using the inner light creatively, we can influence the outcome of situations (the power of the Rod). The 'secret' is always to work from the Ace outwards, and not to seek the direct power of the Nine or Ten without the deeper insights of spiritual reality.

The Nine of Fishes

Fulfilment

The Nine of Water (Cups, Fishes, Direction West) is a card of great blessing. It has physical, emotional, mental and sexual content; it can be the fulfilment of an emotional union, of sexual union, or of a long and productive life. It is a card of fecundity, of production, of reproduction. Its keywords are *Fountain of Full Moon, The Giving Mother, Waters of Life and Love.*

In a sexual and fertile sense, the Nine of Water can be the fulfilment of the womb, the pregnant mother at the outset of her nine-month wait to give birth. It is also the successful birth after the pain and endurance of the Nines of Air and Fire. Upon inner levels, it is the perfection of a full heart, the satisfaction and recognition of a balance and completion. There are strong undertones of giving in this card – the Nine

Fishes swim in a sea of plenty, the Nine Cups are outpouring and ever refilled.

With the Nine of Water, the fusion of will and imagination in the Nine of Fire becomes fluid and flows out into expression. Thus, it is the realization, or making real in manifest terms, of that which we have imagined. Empowered visualization will bring physical results, though they are sometimes unexpected. Fulfilment often comes from surprising sources or directions, and an ideal may be embodied in many different shapes. The greater numbers tend to define forms, but also to increase the number of entities through which energy may be encountered.

The Nine of Beasts

Means

The Nine of Earth (Beasts or Shields, Direction North) shows manifesting energy and ideas taking shape. The power of the Ace of Earth here enables the means towards expression. It is the last step before physical life, and the first step after it. The Nine of Earth is the ninefold inner body that enables the outer form. When the Nine of Beasts appears in tarot patterns, it can suggest means ranging from the most subtle energies to simple physical means towards a chosen end.

Keywords for this number are *Founded within the Earth, The Ninefold Womb, Expressive Moon*. All means towards realization are here: dreams, seeds, life patterns, sexual fertility. These are also the means towards spiritual truth: inner birth, vision, wisdom teachings, and the movement of sexual energy towards subtle ends rather than gratification or physical fertility.

As 3×3 this is the body of the Goddess, the foundation of the all being, the thresholds or crossroads between the

Worlds. All Spheres merge at Nine, the Foundation. But the Earth itself and physical matter in the universe are the outer body of the Goddess, and the Foundation or lunar powers form the subtle body and regenerative force that keeps the outer body in manifestation – and which also demanifests it. The movement between inner and outer is constant and simultaneous.

The Lunar Sphere is centred on the Triad formed of Glory, Victory and Foundation. With the Trumps of The Wheel of Fortune, The Universe, The Fool, The Sun and Moon, we find a potent Ninefold power pattern (see Figure 14). This may be used in meditation for each cycle of Nines in turn.

The Four Tens

The Ten of Birds

Disaster

The Ten of Air (Birds, Swords, Direction East) is the ultimate cut. It is the manifest departure of the flock (the collective entity of any body or situation) and the fall of Ten Blades upon matter. Keywords here would be *Collapsing Form, Cutting Free, The Bitter Wind*. In the Ten, the Ace of Air manifests right through into substance and brings a complete separation, dividing any form or pattern into its constituent parts.

In human terms, this power is often seen as a disaster. It has a special emphasis upon mental and emotional situations, disastrous life events. It can also, of course, indicate physical disasters and natural disasters, and must be interpreted in context of other cards and through the inherent nature of the question, if it appears in a tarot reading.

As a meditational aid, the Ten of Mr helps us to contemplate and understand the inevitability of cycles, of beginnings inherent in endings. The higher Air cards must be understood from within, for if they are encountered as outward forces, they are almost always felt to be hostile or antagonist to our temporary self-interest. If we can turn this situation round, and find their inner meaning, the antagonism or conflict, which is essentially within ourselves, flies away.

The Ten of Air is the transition between night and day; it marks the end of dark comforting night and the dawn of a harsh morning. It often indicates collective disputes and irresolvable difference of opinion, in which acceptance is the key rather than further conflict. Acceptance, is not, however, a meek and diminishing act, but comes from an understanding of the power of Ten, from the knowledge that we must move with it rather than against it.

The Ten of Serpents

Responsibility

The Ten of Fire (Serpents, Rods, Direction South) is the bundle of a manifest will. This implies not only responsibility for our own actions and intent, but often also for the lives and interaction of others. The Ten of Fire is the effect of the intent, imagination, will and energy within the outer world, where we cannot and should not avoid responsibility for our own actions.

Keywords here are *Expressed Intent, Manifest Power, Action and Reaction*. The Ten of Fire, Rods or Serpents is the complex interaction of will, the so-called 'cause and effect' relationship. If our intent is aligned from the Ace, the perfect will of Light, the Ten will be a potent force of balance and control. But if we are separated from the Light within, the Ten of Fire becomes either a burden or the seeming effect of energies and forces *upon* us rather than through us. Whatever we cannot or will not take responsibility for within ourselves seems to come towards us from outside.

This card is also the Earth Dragon, in the sense that we are collectively and individually responsible for the sacred land and planet, and for the forces and other lives upon and within the Earth. The Ten of Serpents can represent the relationship with the subtle fire forces of the land, or it can, in its polar role with the Ten of Beasts, represent work with the land in terms of tools, systems, patterns and projects. These all partake of the Rod, the enabling implement, and the Dragon or Serpent, which is energy expressed in a living form, the power that coils around the Rod.

The Ten of Fishes

Friendship
The Ten of Water (Cups, Fishes, Direction West) is a power of collective Love. It is the inherently friendly nature of our collective existence, our sharing, interacting, creating and living together. It may also refer to specific friendships, depending upon the context of other cards such as the Trumps and Court cards.

Keywords here would be *Great Sharing, Collective Creation, Children of Earth.* The card has a further implication of interchange, of flowing to and fro, of the exchange of energy between people. As a Ten it may refer very simply to the material of our ordinary friendships, but it has inherent within it all the other numbers from the Ace, or power of universal Love. Thus it can refer to that deep spiritual friendship that manifests outwardly, yet does not necessarily include romantic love, sexuality, or other spheres of energy associated with the Element of Water.

As a Ten this card also embodies the essential caring and respect that we should have for our land, for all living creatures on it. We are all fish swimming in the ocean together upon the Mother Earth as she swims through Mother Space, even though hostility divides us against ourselves.

The Ten of Beasts

Opportunity

The Ten of Earth (Beasts, Shields, Direction North) is the ultimate Earth of Earth. It is the planetary body, our own body and all matter/energy. Its keywords would be *Sacred Body, Holy Earth, Perfected Kingdom, Earth Mother, Regenerating Substance.* Tens are numbers of substance, the ultimate expression of all numbers.

The Ten of Beasts offers substantial opportunity, all the material and spiritual opportunity of the world itself. As an Earth card, involved in the manifest body, it has an interesting temporal pattern. We are born into this world as tiny infants, with a lifetime of opportunity ahead of us. As our outer physical body grows and matures, however, the opportunities often seem to peak, and restrictions become increasingly evident in our life pattern. Then, towards the close of a life cycle, the restrictions fall away, and the opportunity of death comes to us.

In a simple sense, the Ten shows opportunity in any situation. It is the Ninefold Gate plus One, the last threshold crossed. All that there is here, and we need only to transform our perceptions to find the opportunities that the Earth Mother offers us.

There is often a special emphasis upon *material* opportunity when this card appears in a reading, depending upon other factors and particularly upon Trumps in association with the Ten.

Now we can move on to look briefly at each of the Court cards or People of the Merlin Tarot.

3

The Court Cards
or People

Introduction to the
Great Court Circle

The Court cards revolve around the Wheel of Life, and have a general relationship to the Directions and Seasons of the year, as shown in Figure 15. This should not be taken literally, but as a poetic or holistic guide to relative qualities and types of person. Providing you do not fall into the trap of using rule-of-thumb attributions – everyone born in November must be a Page of Beasts, everyone born in July a King of Dragons, and so forth – the Great Court Circle can give penetrating insights into People that appear in tarot patterns.

As the relationships are within or of a holism, rather than a linear sequence, I have simply begun the following sequence in the North and travelled around the Circle. As each type of Court card appears for the first time – Page, Warrior, Queen or King – some general information is given. We then progress to the specific type for each Quarter and Element, occasionally comparing them to their polar relatives (see Figure 15).

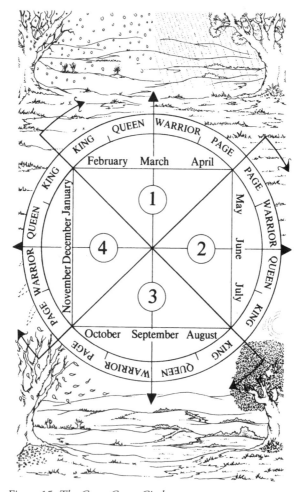

Figure 15: The Great Court Circle

As always with tarot, you will benefit from having the cards in front of you as you read the descriptions, and should aim to rely on your own meditations and insights rather than constantly looking up 'meanings' in a book.

People in the North

The Page of Beasts
Earth of Earth, Male or Female, Keyword: Amenable

The Page of Beasts or Shields is usually a child or younger person. Pages tend to represent individuals before or up to puberty, Warriors tend to represent individuals from puberty to approximately 30 years of age, Queens and Kings, individuals from 30 years onwards. These definitions are very flexible, however, depending entirely upon the inner state of the individual, and not upon physical age.

The keyword for the Page of Beasts is *amenable*, as he or she is of the *expressive* Element of Earth within Earth. This means *plastic* in the original sense of the word, a being that may be shaped and developed. Pages of Beasts tend to be direct, uncomplicated children, mirroring their circumstances and other people around them. Because of this mirroring quality, a Page of Beasts can often innocently reflect truth towards the more complex and confused adult. In the card we see a modest Child holding a mysterious Disc in which the stars are visible.

The Season for this Page is, broadly speaking, late Autumn and early Winter, the Direction North of North West. This is the basic Earth power after the fruit of Autumn, the child of Winter. These Seasons and Direction imply simple waiting, nourishment, development in sleep and Earth-potential. There is also a deeper implication of the natural wisdom of the organism, the waiting soil, the fallen nut, and the watching Fox, shown in the card. This is not conscious, but the innate or inherent power of the Element and Season within the individual. For this type of Page, the coming Spring will eventually cause a blossoming into Warrior status, the inspiring and unstable time of sexual opening and increasing awareness.

If the card indicates a child, as it usually does, it is a being of tremendous potential. The *impressions* made upon and within the Earth or *plastic* soul and mind of this child will be of great influence when he or she emerges into Spring. By comparison we might briefly consider the Page of Birds, of the Element Air, who is wilful, difficult, and not particularly amenable towards or reflective of surrounding people. Earth and Air are 'opposite-opposites' just as Earth and Fire are 'balancing opposites' (see Figure 16 for polarities across and around the Wheel).

The Warrior of Beasts

Air of Earth, Male or Female, Keyword: Ambitious

In the Merlin Tarot the Warriors may be male or female, as was the custom in ancient Celtic culture. But this is not a false pseudo-historical derivation, for it refers to an inner condition rather than to actual combat training or bearing of arms. The Warrior tends to be the status of the young male or female adult, though it can remain present for a lifetime within anyone. There is a broad correlation here to the development of sexuality and the stages of early adulthood, in which many skills of both inner and outer life are learned as

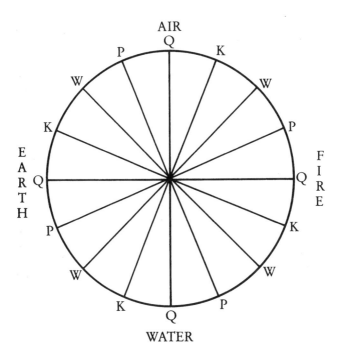

Figure 16: Polarities Around and Across the Wheel

increasingly powerful energies manifest through the body, mind and emotions. The skills balance the inner energies – this is warrior training. In this deeper sense we are all warriors, though many people only develop the minimal, socially conditioned, inner skills during their teenage years, and after that remain relatively static.

The threshold between Warrior and Queen or King status is that obscure but potent crossing point in life at which the individual either slows down and rigidifies, or continues to grow and develop. It can occur during the late teens and early twenties, and many aspects of education and social conditioning tend to freeze the individual at this time. It can also occur in the mid thirties, as people approach the stereotypical false threshold of their middle-life. Both potential thresholds may be happily crossed by people with inner direction, through meditation, visualization and farsight.

The Warrior of Beasts or Shields has the keyword *ambitious*, being of the *originative* Element Air within Earth. The power of Air stirs the potential of Earth into realizing the possibilities of new forms. The ambitions of the Warrior of Beasts range from the most banal to the most extreme, depending upon the factors of imagination and discretion or judgement. This card represents a young man or woman who seeks to benefit from changing his or her circumstances. There is often a corresponding drive to work hard: the Warrior of Beasts will toil and strive for a chosen ambition, determined to bring it to harvest.

The Season of this *persona* is late November, and the Direction approaches true North. The Warrior travels out of the great November threshold marked by the Pleiades (*Samhain*, marked in the modern calendar by what were originally ancestral festivities such as 5 November and Halloween). He or she has seen the harvests that can be obtained in the world, and is determined, with the coming Spring, to work towards such a harvest for the coming year. This is an ambitious person who understands Earth and Winter to be times of labour and preparation for the future, and often has a single-minded attention to specific goals.

In the card we see a Warrior riding upon a huge shire or heavy Horse, the great workhorse of the land. The Warrior seems small, but it is the Horse that is large. The beast offers the power of endurance, strength and connection to the Earth, the living power that works the land. The ambitious Rider is the mind (Air) working with the body (Earth). There is often a desire for material benefit in this type of person, and the ambition is usually self-orientated, though it can be found in altruistic forms. Originally, Warriors worked for the protection and benefit of all people in the land.

Our image shows the earliest phase of this Warrior of Beasts, still bearing the last Sheaf of Corn. The other spiritual animal is the Mouse, providing for the future by storing the seeds of the past.

The Queen of Beasts

Water of Earth, Female, Keyword: Practical

In the Merlin Tarot, Queens are female, and are equal polar partners with the Kings. The Queen is usually a mature woman, with a physical age from the late twenties or early thirties onwards. The *inner* maturity, however, is what defines a Queen or King as distinct from the life-phase of Warrior. Some individuals may merge both phases successfully for several years, others may find a conflict of phase, in which they oscillate between the mature phase of King/Queen and the less mature phase of Warrior. The emergence of a woman as

Queen in tarot always occurs after a certain amount of life experience.

It is worth remembering that the tarot frequently 'chooses' the correct *persona* or Court card, and that they rise within a reading without prejudgement or expectation. Thus, during a lifetime, a particular person may be defined as Page, Warrior and then King or Queen. The sequence does not always follow on through the same Element, and an individual commencing as, say, a Page of Water, may eventually emerge as, say, a King of Fire. The crossing between Element or Directions is enabled by the life powers (Trumps) that come into operation during the life cycle. It can also be radically enabled and empowered by will and intent, working directly with inner transformative exercises and energies.

The Queen of Beasts or Shields has the keyword *practical*, as she is of the *formative* Element, Water, within Earth. She is able to make specific forms out of potential substance, is able to both nourish and define. Her power is that of practical wisdom, the teachings and experience of mature woman on the human level. On the inner level this also involves applied wisdom, the techniques and experiences of spiritual reflection.

In our card she holds a Mirror made from a green Stone, the Stone of Wisdom. Her spiritual animal is the Bear, the creature of the North, of Earth, and of primal Motherhood; here it is shown as a maturing Bear Cub that she protects and rears. Her Direction is somewhat East of North, and her Season is that time between the midwinter solstice and the (old date of) New Year.

On the deepest level, the Queen of Beasts is empowered by Artemis, in her form of the Bear Mother, the Earth Mother. Our image shows the entrance to an Underworld Cave-temple or Long-barrow in the background.

The King of Beasts

Fire of Earth, Male, Keyword: Reliable

Kings in tarot are always male, revealing mature men with considerable power and life experience. There is no value judgement or hierarchy, by the way, in the Court cards – a King is not 'superior' to a Queen, though both King and Queen have greater life experience and maturity than the Warriors and Pages. The Warriors and Pages, from their less defined but more immediate energies, may reveal truth to the Kings or Queens, and may inspire, exhort and catalyse them. As shown in Figures 6 and 15 the key is always one of *interaction* and not of hierarchy or age and gender-defined false authority.

The King of Beasts or Shields has the Direction of North East, and approaches the major threshold of the year, between death and life, Winter and the dawn of earliest Spring, midnight and the beginning of the dark morning phase of a new day. His keyword is *reliable*, as his strength is the strength of the Fire hidden but active within the Earth. He is a mature, dependable and wise male, one upon whom others can, and often do, lay their burdens. But he holds up the Mirror of the Elements (in the card as in life) and teaches that we must all learn balance and strength from within ourselves.

On a deeper level, the King of Beasts is the Earth Father of Winter, the Horned Man. In our image he is crowned and garlanded with Mistletoe, the herb of mysterious sacrifice and regeneration, death that creates life. Thus the King may be relied upon to initiate into the Mysteries of death that brings life, Winter that brings Spring, night that becomes day. His spiritual animal is the Badger, a nocturnal beast of terrible strength, an intelligent, devoted family creature, bearing the alternate light and dark colours of midnight and first dawn, grey, black and white.

The King of Beasts is the primal male ancestor of Earth, and by looking into his Mirror we may contact our own ancestral wisdom. In human terms, he is the older man whom we often instinctively trust, rely upon, and ask for help and advice.

The People of the East

The King of Birds

Fire of Air, Male, Keyword: Severe

The King of Birds, back to back with his rival/partner the King of Beasts, is a mature male. Within him the *creative* Fire radiates through the *originative*, inspiring, changeable Element of Air. He is characterized by the keyword *severe*, for the cutting power of the Sword of Air reaches its ultimate phase of creative control and will in this *persona*.

Severity in this King is just rather than unjust, and as a human being he is often involved with matters of justice, discipline, civic and personal order. His Direction is at the threshold of the year, associated with the month of February and the ancient feast of Imbolc. The King of Birds or Swords brings vitality and beginnings out of the cold of Winter, and epitomizes the clean cutting power of a new blade. He may also be that type of inspirer and teacher who enables us to see the value of severity and discipline within ourselves, ranging from the skills of the mind to the spiritual arts. Most of all he teaches us what we must lose, leading us to peaks beyond which we cannot retain a concept of false selfhood.

In the card we see the King of Birds seated on a Throne of Glass upon a high Mountain top. He carries the Sword of the East, and his spiritual animal is the Eagle. As a deeper power, he fuses certain primal god forms, or perhaps (like all Court cards) he represents a god form out of which later deities known to history have become defined and differentiated. He is, for example, the kingly power of justice to which the supplicant applies, even at the risk of self. He is also a power of flight and communication, swiftness, accuracy. In our image there are flocks of Birds flying across a Winter Landscape: they are the messengers of the King of Air, heralding swift movement, the beginning of Seasons, and the power of individual thoughts transforming collective consciousness.

The Queen of Birds

Water of Air, Female, Keyword: Serious

The Queen of Birds or Swords is an older woman, the feminine counterpart of the King in many ways. Her *formative* energy, often associated with the emotions, works through the *originative* power of Air to give a *serious persona*. Thus she will criticize emotional outbursts, and will tend to use the Sword, her mental discipline, to balance emotions within herself.

In the card she holds Sword and Scabbard equally in prominence: her formative, feminine energy balances the originative Sword. This is one of the Grail Mysteries, that the Sword and Scabbard should never be separated or regarded as superior to one another. As a deeper image, the Queen of Birds is the stern but fair feminine power, able to both give and take. Her Direction is the East, her Season early Spring, in which the frost can still cut off the budding leaf. Just as the

King is upon the aery threshold of the Mountain tops, where the heights aspire to light and Air, so is the Queen upon the high Cliff-tops of the Sea, where Air and Water meet.

Her spiritual creatures are sea birds, and in the foreground of the image we see a Nest with two Eggs in it. The Queen guards with Sword and Scabbard the potential life about to emerge from the Water of the Egg into the Air of Spring.

The Warrior of Birds

Air of Air, Male or Female, Keyword: Combative

The Warrior of Birds or Swords is a young man or woman in whom the *originative* Air is doubled, giving rising to a turbulent and changeable nature. This person is enthusiastic, highly active, always rushing, often argumentative. He or she may be buffeted to and fro by the winds of energy within, rushing from one enthusiasm to another, ready to fight and defend ideals and beliefs.

The keyword here is *combative*, and the urge to combat may either be exteriorized or remain as an inner conflict. The Season is Spring, and the Direction is due East. In the card we see the Warrior, youth or maiden, riding a spirited white Horse that is free of Reins, though Reins are present. The Warrior draws a Bow shooting ahead of the gallop. The spiritual creature is a Swift or Swallow with darting flight and shrill cry.

Upon a deeper level, this is the androgynous god of beginning, rising energies, intense feelings and powerful ideas. It can also be the young warrior god or goddess, riding to right imbalances. There is a further correlation here with the young Diana or Apollo, god and goddess of the hunt, of prophecy, music, archery and healing.

The Page of Birds

Earth of Air, Male or Female, Keyword: Difficult

The Page of Birds or Swords is a child or younger person, usually below the early teens in age. This person has the *expressive* Earth within the *originative* Air, and can have inner conflicts that will only be resolved with maturity and experience. Sometimes it is a child wise beyond his or her years, but lacking the means or experience to relate to such wisdom.

The Direction is South East, a child of Spring moving into Summer. The keyword is *difficult*, and the difficult nature can show in several different ways. It often manifests as obstinacy, a kind of inner strength and wilfullness. The Page of Air can also be the intelligent child, perceptive beyond his or years, to whom less intelligent adults (such as schoolteachers) have no adequate response. Such Pages are often inspired (Air) by a wise teacher (Earth), if they are fortunate enough to meet one. They often have demanding natures and special needs.

Our card shows the Page armed with a large Bow as yet undrawn, also a full Quiver of Arrows and a sharp Dagger. We see that the Bow is just about to come off his/her shoulder, showing readiness for action.

The People in the South

The Court of the South consists of Fire People, people with a summery quality, powerful will and great radiant energy. There is often a charismatic or sexual aura about people in the South, due to the potency of their Inner Fire. In this significant area of energy we must be aware that spiritual enlightenment, charisma and sexual power are all one; they derive from differing patterns or direction of the Inner Fire. The Element of Fire is associated with creativity, and People of the South are often superb creative artists, for they combine the inner power with the will and discipline and balance of the Rod and Dragon.

The Page of Serpents

Earth of Fire, Male or Female, Keyword: Diligent

The Page of Serpents or Rods is a child or young person full of potential, bursting with energy. The *expressive* Earth combined with *creative* Fire makes this child confident and willing to work very hard if necessary. The keyword is *diligent*, and the diligence will be applied in any work, from ordinary daily activities to creative expression.

The card shows the Page about to run, bearing a short Wand or Staff, the token of the messenger who carries a given authority. Whatever this person undertakes will be done in an unassuming, efficient manner. The spiritual animal is a baby Dragon, just beginning to emit its first flames, experimenting with its Inner Fire.

The Season for this Page is May, and the Direction is South East. The Page stands upon the threshold of Summer, for May Day, marked by the Pleiades and the feast of Beltane, is the beginning of Summer. Thus the Page of Serpents is the young god/goddess of the new Summer, ready to run to the heights of the full southern Sun, shining upon the Hilltops of our image. We see that the Page is already in the Uplands, and ready to run higher, up the Slope rising from left to right (East to South).

The Summer child is often a redhead, though we need not be too literal when this card appears in a tarot pattern.

The fiery *qualities* of the redheaded boy or girl are indicated here, if not an actual *persona* with red hair. In very early times, dating back to the megalithic culture from which the Celts inherited much of their stellar and Underworld lore, the redhead was a sacred person, often chosen as king or queen. But the way to Queen or King begins with a Page or young soul.

The Warrior of Serpents

Air of Fire, Male or Female, Keyword: Perceptive

The Warrior of Serpents or Rods is the enlivener and protector of the Summer land, a person from the early teens to late twenties with endless vitality, ceaseless activity and ability. The *originative* power of Air and *creative* Fire give him/her intuitive insight (not necessarily born of experience, but arising spontaneously). The keyword here is *perceptive*, for the Warrior is able to see to the heart of any person or situation.

In the card, the masked Warrior rides upon a healthy chestnut Horse, the beast of Epona, horse goddess of the South. The Warrior of Serpents carries a long Spear at rest, for s/he knows instinctively how to control aggression or combative energies within. The Mask is an ancient emblem of the South, and the Warrior is still masked because he/she is potent but inexperienced; the inner light is masked by the outer form. With the Queen and King the outer mask is removed, and the face shows the light within.

The Direction is approaching due South, the month late May or early June, leading to the Summer solstice when day is longest. The spiritual animal is the Serpent, sacred to the Fire deities such as Apollo or the Celtic Brig or Brigid.

The Warrior of the South is often a skilled facilitator, able to pierce the heart of a situation and bring it to balance with the necessary action. If s/he couches the Spear or throws it, the results are dramatic, but the preferred action is often to mediate and simply show potential rather than to impose it.

The Queen of Serpents

Water of Fire, Female, Keyword: Skilful

The Queen of Serpents or Rods is a powerful mature woman, often of great sexual attraction. We must, however, be cautious in using the term 'sexual attraction', for it does not necessarily mean stereotypical glamour. The Queen of Serpents is, however, a person of *formative* Water and *creative* Fire, hence she may be powerfully sexual. The energies may also be routed into creative work such as art or music, or into a career, a lifetime dedication to developing, nourishing and bringing into being something of value.

The Direction is West of South, just beyond the peak of midsummer, and the Season the months of late June and early July. The Inner Fire is very strong in the Queen, and her fusion of fiery and watery nature can lead to powerful impulsive urges. Usually, she is able to balance these with her will and experience. The keyword is *skilful*, for she is the Queen of Rods, able to mediate, balance, control, manipulate and direct energy.

Our card shows the Queen seated upon a serpent Throne, in the mountainous Uplands towards which we originally saw the Page about to run. Behind her is a dormant Volcano, which may erupt at any time. Her wand is a fusion of the Staff or Rod and blossoming Flower – traditionally this is a violet-coloured bloom, showing formative lunar powers harmonized with creative solar fire.

In her hand the Queen of Fire bears a tiny Lizard, basking in the full sunlight. Her spiritual animal is the Cat. In our card, the hair of both Cat and Queen is red, flame-coloured.

The King of Serpents

Fire of Fire, Male, Keyword: Decisive

The King of Serpents or Rods is a mature male, one in whom the potential of inner and outer being is well harmonized. As Fire of Fire, he is powerful, creative and well-balanced. He is an individual of very strong will and ceaseless energy. He may also, rarely, be a highly empowered spiritual being, but we must always exercise caution in this interpretation, as false 'gurus' often try to present themselves as Kings of Fire. The genuine Summer King lacks pretension, only having inner light and harmony. As a rule, this type of person does not seek us out, but we may find him if we are drawn towards his energy.

The Direction is West of South, the ripe time of Summer, as July turns into August. At the very threshold of the Quarter, where the King sits back to back with the King of Fishes, he is *Bel* and *Lugh* in the old Celtic mythology, the god of light, fire and high places. The August festival of Lammas (Lughnasadh) is named after this major deity.

In the card, the King is shown seated upon a dragon Throne, at the shore of burning golden Lake. He is crowned with a Dragon and Flames, and his Robe is of gold and flame pattern, partly revealed through the parting of his red Cloak. In his right hand he carries a long pointed Staff of spiralling pattern, and his left hand is held open in a sign of welcome. His face, like that of all the Kings and Queens, is unmasked. Just beyond the Throne is a golden Tripod with a Salamander, the legendary Fire creature, within its basin.

The keyword is *decisive*, as all decisions made by the King are balanced and fired or empowered from within. He is able to decide on proper action without debate or reflection, and works directly from inner enlightenment and creative power. Coiled upon a rock at his feet is a Snake, the spiritual animal of sacred Fire within the sacred body, be it the human body or the body of the land or planet.

The People in the West

West is the Direction of the feelings, of Love, of the Element of Water. It is also the Direction and power of fertility in all senses, either as the spiritual Love that generates the universe, or as the collective or individual fertility of motherhood. The People of the West live in and through their emotions, and are often giving and forgiving individuals. Upon the higher octaves of the West, emotion is transformed into spiritual power, selfless love, compassion, even sacrifice. The Court of the West is concerned with purification, cleansing, regeneration, nourishment and support. These, too, are the qualities of the People.

West is the Direction of the Fortunate Isles, or Blessed Otherworld, the setting sun. People of the West can often enter that Otherworld through their sensitivities, feelings and spiritual insights and devotions. They can also communicate this vision and the presence of the spiritual world to others (the power of the Cup).

The King of Fishes

Fire of Water, Male, Keyword: Jovial

Back to back with the King of Serpents is the King of Fishes. These Kings of Fire and Water support one another and are partners upon the thresholds of the Autumn, both being involved in high levels of energy, one of Fire and Light, the other of Water and Love.

The King of Fishes or Cups is a mature male with considerable life experience, and he has not been hardened or embittered by his life. The *creative* Fire within him is modified and made gentle by the *formative* water, his main Element. The keyword for this person is *jovial*, which means more than merely good-natured or jolly. The god Jove or Jupiter was the ancient All-Father, the giving god from whom all bounty and kindness flowed. He is associated with compassion and mercy upon the Tree of Life (see Figure 2), and one of the most constant factors in the King of Fishes is his compassionate, giving nature. As King, however, he is able to temper this with the power of Fire, and does not let his kindly feelings control him or carry him away, as is true with the Warrior of Fishes, whom we shall meet shortly.

The Direction is West of South, and at the beginning of August, the theme is of first fruitfulness and beginning of harvest. The Water Element gives a particular emphasis to feeling and emotions, the fruits of creativity, 'fatherhood' in both the spiritual and material sense.

In the card we see the King at the Sea-shore, the realm where all Elements meet and where Water predominates. He sits upon a granite Throne that is clearly washed or even covered by the tides at times, for there are Sea Creatures around it and lodged upon it. This gives us some insight into the

King's nature, for even the highest tide that washes his Throne will not carry him away. His face is smiling and welcoming, kind and compassionate. In his hands he bears a glass Vessel. His spiritual creatures are the Crab, the tenacious beast that crosses between land and water, and the Dolphin, the highly intelligent and friendly animal of the ancient sea gods.

The King of Fishes' hair is plaited, unlike that of his Elemental polar opposite, the King of Birds, whose locks blow wildly in the wind. Plaiting hair is an ancient magical technique, for it involves twisting or sealing up power. In our image the plaited hair indicates that the King chooses to restrain his full power out of kindliness, but he can, like the sea-gods of old, unleash the storm if he chooses. In human terms, this individual is full of hidden depths (Water) and deep currents, seldom revealing his true strength, working through gentleness rather than overt acts of will.

On a deeper level, we may link this King to certain primal water deities, to the speed and intelligence of the dolphin, sea-friend of humanity, the jovial or all-giving power, with the potential for great storms.

The Queen of Fishes

Water of Water, Female, Keyword: Loving

The Queen of Fishes or Cups is a mature woman with deep sexual and fertility powers. These may manifest as actual motherhood, or through a creative line of work. This woman is often in love, giving her heart freely, revealing the power of love to those involved with her. As a mother she is devoted and protective, as a lover she is both fulfilling and demanding.

The *formative* power of Water is redoubled with in her, and everything in her life is about nourishment, sexual exchange, giving and receiving, feeling, passion. Her keyword is *loving* in all senses. As she grows older, the sexual side of her nature may be less apparent, but it never fades away. Many Queens of Water become spiritually dedicated later in their lives. In earlier cultures they might have become saints or holy women, replacing the bodily love with the spiritual, and realizing that they are indeed one Love. The older Queen of Cups may also become the mother of an extended family, the grandmother in a spiritual or physical sense of many younger people, all treated equally as her children.

The Queen's Direction is due West, the time of the Autumn equinox and the great tides. She is also associated with Venus, the evening star, and the power of the lunar cycles. These forces tend to be strong within any woman represented by this card.

In our image, we see her sitting upon a huge shell Throne with the Sea washing around her. It seems as if the Waters flow up and become her Robe, embroidered with a pattern of tiny fishes. In her left arm she cradles the Horn, the magical implement of fertility, or vitality, of sexuality, of summoning. Her spiritual animal is the Seal, reminding us of the ancient traditions that seals are the People of the Sea, often associated with the Fairy Realm and the magical singing of the West that lures men into the unknown.

Upon a deeper or mythic level, she may be identified, to a certain extent, with Aphrodite in classical myth, but the Queen of Cups is also a Sea-Mother, so she combines the sea-functions in one figure.

The Warrior of Fishes

Air of Water, Male or Female, Keyword: Idealistic

The Warrior of Fishes or Cups is a young man or woman filled with dreams, visions and high expectations of life. The *originative* power of Air stirs the *formative* Element of Water, causing the Warrior's emotions to be highly developed. The keyword is *idealistic*: often an ideal will replace simple human love within this person. With experience, such idealism is often modified, but is never completely abandoned or lost.

The Direction is North of West, after the Autumn equinox towards the close of September and early October. In the card we see the young man or woman riding upon a white Horse, sign of idealism and purity of intent. The Warrior has let go of the Reins (for a dream will be more empowering than common sense or control of energies), and offers a Cup to the sky. The Horse wades through the incoming Sea proudly, and although the Warrior has a Shield (sign of approaching Winter in the North), he/she does not bear it up, and carries no other arms. In the distance we see Whales rising from the ocean; these spiritual creatures indicate the tremendous power of the Element of Water that resides within the Warrior, mostly hidden, yet surfacing from time to time for Air.

The Page of Fishes

Earth or Water, Male or Female, Keyword: Pleasant

The Page of Fishes or Cups is a young person or child, probably before the age of puberty. This is a responsive, easy child, very attached to parents, and able to make friends with others (in contrast to the Page of Birds, who can find making friendships difficult). The *expressive* Earth and *formative* Water make this Page a generally good-natured person, as Water and Earth merge imperceptibly into one another. The keyword is *pleasant*.

The Direction is North of West, in October, just before the threshold that crosses into Winter. In our card the late Autumn Landscape is set by the Sea, but the Tide has yet to rise, for this Page is Earth of Water. Again we see the Crab as a spiritual creature, and in the distance a flock of Sea Birds come to land. The Page holds a copper Bowl (Venus) from which a tiny Fish leaps. The small Fish is his/her personal creature, for if it is nourished and allowed to grow the Page will begin to move around the Court Circle and change *persona*.

Table of Court Cards or People in the Merlin Tarot

Page (male or female)	Element of Earth	Child
Warrior (male or female)	Element of Air	Young adult
Queen (female)	Element of Water	Mature adult
King (male)	Element of Fire	Mature adult

4
Methods of Divination, Farsight and Insight

Before proceeding to examples in which cards are laid out and interpreted, we should briefly consider each of the three categories within which such applications of tarot are found. The categories are: 1: Divination; 2: Farsight; 3: Insight. Each category may be seen as a mode of consciousness; each mode of consciousness corresponds to functions of the individual psyche, the collective or ancestral consciousness, and the Three Worlds of Lunar, Solar and Stellar relativity. The Three Worlds generate and enfold all life, all aspects of consciousness and energy, from material substance to metaphysical entities; such is the foundation of the world view of tarot.

We may apply the cosmology shown within tarot to form patterns for divination, farsight or insight in addition to using single, paired, triadic or other number combinations of images (cards). The Trumps Moon, Sun and Star define three levels or degrees of consciousness, with three threshold Trumps of Fortune, Justice and Judgement.

Thus, so-called 'divination' may reflect energies or interactions upon three levels:

1 *The Wheel of Fortune:* events in the outer or consensual world of human and environmental relationships.

2 *Justice:* events in the inner creative world of spiritual energies.

3 *Judgement:* events in the cosmic, stellar or supernal world. In divination this third mode may also represent collective consciousness, or long-term cycles of events involving nations, races and metaphysical cycles of development.

Divination

Various methods of divination are described shortly, but before any use of these is made, we should define some of the properties or behaviour of tarot in actual divinatory practice.

Tarot cannot work for us as humans to divine matters upon a cosmic or universal scale. There is no point is asking questions relating to the life of the solar system and expecting tarot patterns to provide an answer; such questions are matters of metaphysical or mystical vision rather than of mere divination. We may use tarot Trumps or patterns in meditation to aid our understanding of reality, but this is not a matter of divination or prediction, as it relates to higher modes of consciousness.

The broader the range of the query, the more archetypical will be the responding pattern of symbols. A crude example should demonstrate this operational matter. There is little or no point in asking 'Will there be war?', as war and conflict are an enduring aspect of human suffering in the outer world—wars express our imbalance, ranging from individual to collective energies and follies. The reply to such a general (pointless) question will be cards which symbolize the energies concerned in an archetypical and broad manner; it will be difficult to define a meaningful temporal answer.

For precise divination we need to ask if there will be a

conflict of defined nature between specified parties within a selected time period. Only such a firmly attuned, precise mode of forming questions will generate detailed answers; it will result in some identical cards to the more vague question discussed above, but there will be supportive elements in the pattern which will enable the reader to be more precise in interpretation.

The divinatory power of tarot operates only in the context of questions that relate to matters below the Abyss (see Figure 2). The Abyss, which is physically the distance between our solar system and any other or, metaphysically, the distance between human consciousness and divine or originative consciousness, is one of the paradoxes of mystical perception: it is a barrier of seemingly insurmountable proportions, yet there are well-known ways of crossing it in either direction. Divination is not one of the Paths across the Abyss, though a higher mode of divination, that of prophecy, may bridge the Abyss occasionally.

There is another way of expressing the law of divination in connection with tarot: the cards may reveal insights into both inner and outer events/energies, but they will not reveal deeper truths other than through meditation. The quality of revelation is entirely dependent upon the consciousness and intent of the individual using the tarot symbols; more insight or truth may be gained through a short period of right meditation than through many hours of tedious sequences of laying out cards for divination.

Farsight

Farsight is traditionally employed to overlook situations at a distance from the observer. This does not usually involve a predictive or divinatory function; the pattern of tarot symbols is generated to define a current interplay of factors or energies in a known location. A typical example would be one in which the tarot reader seeks general information on the status of a distant friend; a question of this sort may be answered through symbols extending into the material, mental, emotional and spiritual levels of the situation defined within the query.

More complex situations may be overlooked by farsight with tarot patterns, but it is often difficult to obtain factual material responses to queries involving such situations. The more complex a situation, such as one with a large number of persons or potential interactions, the more abstract the response will be. This is simply because tarot always tends towards truth; in this matter we touch upon one of the most important aspects of tarot in connection with divination, farsight and insight.

Tarot always works towards the true heart of any query, even if this is counter to the formulated question that is uppermost in the mind of the seeker. This quality can be very frustrating for beginners with tarot, but with some practice becomes an invaluable factor for the individual who seeks enduring insights through work with tarot symbols. A general rule, never to be side-stepped, is that while we should define each question as fully possible, we should never limit or force the answers by imposing conditions or preconceptions upon them. It may seem initially that we impose such preconceptions by detailed formulation of the query, but the inherent tendency of tarot symbols to gravitate towards the heart of any matter will frequently cut through this initial structure.

In this context it would be extremely difficult, if not impossible, to use farsight for trivial matters such as industrial or military espionage; the symbolic language of tarot simply does not relate to such matters in direct terms, or in sufficient serial detail to be of any value. In personal, mental, emotional and spiritual matters, however, tarot can and does provide unfailing responses to defined questions involving farsight.

Insight

Insight is the result of higher functions of tarot. These functions interact with human consciousness through the disciplined arts of meditation, visualization, and contemplation. Our descriptions of the individual Trumps deal mainly with insights into the symbols and their relationship with one another, and with deeper insights into their function as a holism or model of the universe. Insight comes from work with tarot over periods of time, yet the actual moments of insight are timeless.

Results from divination, farsight and insight will vary enormously. The variation is more noticeable in the lesser arts of divination and farsight; the closer we work with the world of expressed interactions (the everyday world), the more variable will our collections of defining symbols (cards in layouts) become. Some card sequences are utterly clear as soon as they are laid out, others may require lengthy meditation. The art is greatly enhanced and made more rapid by regular meditation upon the Trumps in their own right the more trivial the reader's relationship to the symbols, the more random and chaotic their appearance will be in any attempts to generate a meaningful pattern for any chosen purpose.

A skilled meditator with experience of tarot will be able to generate accurate patterns of divination and farsight with a very small number of cards. Many methods in publication tend towards large sequences of cards, but these are not necessary. Our basic *Three Rays* method, outlined in the next chapter, can be worked with as few as four cards, though it may be expanded to seven or twelve if required.

Tarot Pattern Making

The entire subject of randomizing, shuffling and laying out is central to the minor arts of tarot, and may under certain circumstances run over into the major arts. We may define the minor and major arts as follows:

MINOR ARTS: 1. Divination, 2. Farsight, 3. Personal insight.
MAJOR ARTS: 4. Meditation, 5. Visualization, 6. Contemplation, 7. Pattern making and story-telling.

This definition covers seven arts, all of which are encompassed by the highest art, that of pattern making or story-telling.

To establish a working relationship between ourselves and the tarot, we must first examine and meditate upon the actual process of shuffling and laying out cards, for this has a symbolic content that is often ignored or trivialized. When we randomize a tarot pack we are *dissolving the universe.* Conversely, when we lay out a pattern after randomizing the pack, we are *creating the universe.* When the pack lies dormant, it is the universe in potential. This is an important concept fundamental to tarot either as picture symbols or as images within a mystical tradition, yet it is frequently ignored, and further confused by various theories regarding statistical correlations, or temporal suspension. Tarot patterns are primarily *magical rituals* rather than attempts to isolate sets of meaningful symbols in any coincidental order of appearance.

In other words, it is the pattern or layout that is important in tarot, and not the ever-changing presentation of symbols within that pattern. This is sometimes a difficult concept to grasp, for the cycle of images (cards turned up) is always the focus of outer attention and interest; but on inner levels it is the matrix or pattern that creates the appearance of those specific orders of cards. This paradoxical theory will be unacceptable to anyone who believes that tarot works through statistics or random number sequences, for it defies superficial logic.

Once we have understood the principle of *creation and dissolution* with tarot, much confusion over handling and reading sets of cards disappears. The process of shuffling or randomizing cards is an outer ritual, an expression of the metaphysical reality that dissolves the worlds; all previous combinations and interactions are separated, and the elements or energies are present in potential. This potential state is a randomized pack, face down, cleared of any associations.

When the reader lays out cards according to a cosmological pattern, he or she enacts an ancient magical ritual, a minute reflection of divine creation. There are two ways of developing this concept in practice. The first is that a willed pattern, regardless of its tradition or origin, will give meaning and insight to any random cards that appear within it. This is perhaps the most acceptable rationalization in modern psychological terms. Even if this alone was all that occurred in tarot work, it would be a valuable and effective system of symbolic insight and experiment. There is, however, much more to tarot than may be rationalized in personal or psychic terms. The second development, of creation or pattern making concepts, runs through esoteric traditions using tarot images.

Dissolving

The act of dissolution or disassembly is an essential first stage to any successful tarot work. The reader/meditator should commence by balancing and stilling his or her awareness. This is a basic meditational exercise, and should be undertaken in its own right, unconnected to any religious, magical or meditative school or cult. It is the primal act of meditation – just as poetically the universe originates in the void, so does consciousness originate out of nothing. A stilling and meditative clearing of consciousness should be undertaken before any operation with tarot, be it divination or further meditation.

Next we make a *physical representation* of this inner act of stillness; this is where the magical ritual of tarot is outwardly evident. We shuffle or randomize the cards, and when we do so we are (consciously or even unconsciously) ritualizing the dissolution of the universe. Sets of interaction between the Four Elements are separated or stilled, reaching inwards to potential being, ultimately stemming from non-being. The non-being is truly found within our deepest selves, that point beyond which all consciousness dissolves; the potential being is represented (for the duration of the ritual) by the tarot pack or cycle.

It is possible, in theory, for an experienced meditator to 'clear' a tarot pack without shuffling, but the physical ritual of dissolving any previous order within the cards is central to tarot symbolism in practice. One of the most effective ways of clearing a pack, particularly during a session of pattern making, is as follows.

Clearing

1   The pack is divided and laid out face down into seven groups or packets in a single line. This is done by holding the pack, and building the seven packets sequentially, working from one to seven, left to right, laying down a single card upon each position until the pack is reduced to one remaining card ($7 \times 11 = 77$), which may be placed anywhere. There are various metaphysical and mathematical correlations in this procedure, relating to the Worlds, Spheres and planets, with the remaining card representing The Fool, but these concepts are not essential in any way to the practical operation of clearing a pack.

2   The seven packets, now containing all of the pack fully randomized, are placed upon one another, working from left to right, and recombined into a single pack. This sequence will clear any connections between cards, either physical/statistical or energetic/intuitive.

Shuffling

The reader holds the pack of cleared cards and defines a question, attuning his or her previously stilled awareness to the subject. This is a meditative process, and not a matter of force, wishing or will power.

The pack is then shuffled in the normal manner, but slowly and steadily. A steady pace (quite different to the fast shuffle of card games) allows the reader to stop easily at any given point in the shuffling sequence. Steady rhythmic shuffling is a physical reiteration of the turning of the Wheel (for both the cosmology and psychology of tarot are based upon Three Wheels or Spirals of consciousness). With practice and meditation upon tarot, a reader will know intuitively when to stop shuffling and lay out cards. With continued use, this inner sense becomes highly developed, and in some cases the cards will seem to 'kick' or lock immovably at the right point in a steady shuffling process. If shuffling is too rapid, this intuitive process may be disrupted when the cards run beyond the point required.

There is no point in expecting your cards to act physically in a manner which obviates general laws; we are not suggesting any dramatic psycho-kinetic event. The 'kick' results from a fusion of meditative consciousness with ritual pattern making. Some people never experience a 'kick' from the cards, yet always stop shuffling, intuitively, in the best possible place for the purposes of their reading or layout of patterns. Intuition is the key to the moment of pausing and laying out, rather than mathematical number sequences or rigid rules of practice. The formalizing, or pattern making, comes *after* dissolution, shuffling and intuition. Thus, we fill a pattern (the method of layout chosen and applied by the reader) with consciousness symbolized by images chosen intuitively. With practice the general term 'intuition' may be replaced by recognized levels of consciousness reaching through the Three Worlds and their thresholds formed by the Three Wheels.

Systems of Divination, Farsight and Insight

The Merlin Tarot may be used in the same way as any other tarot pack, according to systems or methods preferred by the user. But there are a number of previously unpublished

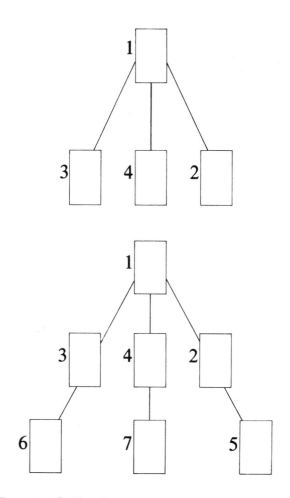

Figure 17: The Three Rays

methods of use which relate specifically to this pack, and to the Mysteries of Merlin.

Please note: Reversed cards are not used in any of the following patterns, as the Merlin Tarot is a balanced deck of images. If any cards appear in reverse, simply lay them the right way up into your pattern.

The Three Rays

In this simple but effective method of using the cards, the primal symbol of the Three Rays or Three Strands is employed. The triple pattern represents the basic polarities of positive, negative and balanced, or male, female, androgyne. In druidic tradition and mystical perception, three rays or primal qualities of divine consciousness interact to form the created worlds through their rotation in a Fourfold Cycle. This symbol is shown as the Three Strands from the Distaff of the Weaver Goddess in our Trump Judgement. The rotation or spinning of Three Rays or Strands forms the Three Worlds and their limits or thresholds, the Three Wheels. But as always, we should see this pattern of Worlds and Wheels as three turnings of a triple spiral, reaching from origination to expression, or from Crown to Kingdom.

The Three Rays pattern is shown in Figure 17, and can be worked using only four cards. The cards are cleared, shuffled, and the first four laid out face down in the pattern and order illustrated. They are then turned face up displayed and read as follows:

1   Represents the seed, heart or root of the query.
2   Represents positive aspects or energies within the situation.
3   Represents negative aspects or energies within the situation.

4 Represents the fusion of the first three cards, and the result or outcome or basic answer to the query.

A more detailed development of this pattern is to repeat the layout three times, until twelve cards are displayed. The three sets of cards (3×3 Rays/but 3×4 cards) may be defined as follows:

1st set: Past relating to the query.
2nd set: Present relating to the query.
3rd set: Future relating to the query.

Alternative Pattern of Three Rays
A more sophisticated pattern based upon the Three Ray concept uses seven cards as shown in Figure 17. This employs only one cycle or layout (as opposed to the pattern of one or three layouts described above), but has a more complex and comprehensive interpretation.

Positions 1–4 represent inner spiritual and transpersonal matters; positions 5–7 represent outer temporal and personal matters. Position 4 acts as the central or pivotal point between personal and transpersonal consciousness.

1 Seed or root (transpersonal).
2 Positive.
3 Negative.
4 Resolution, balance, or centre.
5 Positive (personal).
6 Negative.
7 Outcome.

This sevenfold pattern within Three Rays has a broad correspondence to a septenary pattern of Moon, Sun, Star and planets or polar Trumps as follows:

1 Star (spiritual consciousness, deepest impulses and energies, Trump of The Star).
2 Jupiter (transpersonal positive, giving energies, Trump of The Emperor).
3 Mars (transpersonal negative, taking energies, Trump of Death).
4 Sun (fusion of transpersonal and personal central harmonious balancing energies, Trump of The Sun).
5 Venus (positive emotional, giving aspects of personality, Trump of The Empress).
6 Mercury (negative analytic, intellectual aspects of personality, related to image of Minerva, Trump of The Chariot).
7 Moon (fusion, outcome, generation of events/consciousness from all of the foregoing, Trump of The Moon).

In patterns such as the sevenfold system, there is an obvious implication that a Trump appearing in its own position (e.g. The Emperor in position 2) has a strengthened effect, while a Trump appearing in its polar opposite position (e.g. Death in position 2) has a cancelling or negative effect upon the consciousness/energies of that position.

We could extend this conceptual model and include the Court cards, for they express Elemental energies as *personae* in abstract, ranging from god forms to psychological types, and have a concrete function in card reading as symbols for actual persons or personalities. Thus, a Queen of Birds in position S (an analytical, stern, active person in the position of The Empress) might modulate or even conflict with the basic energies/consciousness of the position.

Much of this subtlety of reading comes with practice, and once the basic attributes of each card have been *learned* (rather than read from books or lists), the reader soon develops a style and feeling for the relationships defined.

The Spindle

In this method of laying out tarot, the Spindle is used as a pattern. Card positions are allocated according to the Trumps of the Spindle as shown in Figure 18, and seven cards are laid out in order after clearing and shuffling the pack.

The three divisions of the pattern broadly represent: 1. the origin of the query, 2. energies at work in the query situation, and 3. the outcome of the query.

Positions on the Spindle
The Upper Third
A. The Star.
B. Judgement.
C. Justice.

These positions, named after the Trumps that define the energies/consciousness of the upper third of the Spindle, represent (A–B) spiritual impulses/transtemporal or transpersonal situations and energies. They may also indicate (B) collective or world movements of consciousness, far-reaching changes that affect the individual or situation of the query, and may indicate effects carried over from the distant past. They correspond to the Stellar World, with *Justice* (C) acting as a threshold to the Solar World.

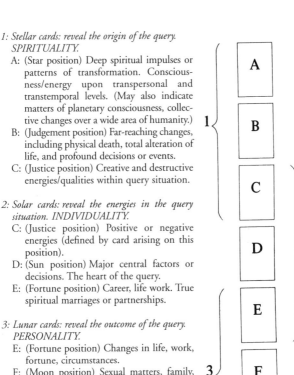

1: Stellar cards: reveal the origin of the query. SPIRITUALITY.

   A: (Star position) Deep spiritual impulses or patterns of transformation. Consciousness/energy upon transpersonal and transtemporal levels. (May also indicate matters of planetary consciousness, collective changes over a wide area of humanity.)

   B: (Judgement position) Far-reaching changes, including physical death, total alteration of life, and profound decisions or events.

   C: (Justice position) Creative and destructive energies/qualities within query situation.

2: Solar cards: reveal the energies in the query situation. INDIVIDUALITY.

   C: (Justice position) Positive or negative energies (defined by card arising on this position).

   D: (Sun position) Major central factors or decisions. The heart of the query.

   E: (Fortune position) Career, life work. True spiritual marriages or partnerships.

3: Lunar cards: reveal the outcome of the query. PERSONALITY.

   E: (Fortune position) Changes in life, work, fortune, circumstances.

   F: (Moon position) Sexual matters, family, home, children. Also unconscious foundational aspects of personality within query.

   G: (World/Universe position) The physical outcome or pattern of the query. Outer activities, temporal relationships or partnerships. Manifestation of consciousness/energies defined in higher positions of the Spindle.

Figure 18: The Spindle

The Middle Third

C. Justice.

D. The Sun.

E. The Wheel of Fortune.

These positions, named after the Trumps that define energies/consciousness in the middle third of the Spindle, represent (C) the interaction of positive and negative energies at work in the query situation. They indicate (C–D) creative and destructive forces or patterns of consciousness in life, and indicate some powerful long-term life situations, though others are indicated by the upper third of the Spindle. Position D represents the heart of the query and inner core or heart of the person or persons concerned. Positions D–E major decisions, individuality, and matters of career, life work, marriages and partnerships. The middle third relates to the Solar World, with The Wheel of Fortune acting as a threshold into the Lunar World.

The Lower Third

E. The Wheel of Fortune.

F. The Moon.

G. Earth (The Fool or World).

These positions represent (E) daily changes of fortune in life and work situations and immediate short-term circumstances, also the emotional and mental condition or impulses of the querent or subjects of the query; (F) natural life factors, biological and health conditions, inherited tendencies, the dream or unconscious life; (G) personality, family, home, place of work, temporal or temporary relationships and situations. The lower third generally indicates the outcome of the query.

We may see a broad correspondence to the planets in the seven positions of the Spindle as follows:

1　Uranus and Pluto (1st Sphere on the Tree of Life and the Abyss with its mysterious bridge).
2　Neptune and Saturn (2nd and 3rd Spheres).
3　Mars and Jupiter (4th and 5th Spheres).
4　Sol (6th Sphere).
5　Venus and Mercury (7th and 8th Spheres).
6　Luna (9th Sphere).
7　Earth (10th Sphere).

Seven cards are sufficient for a very detailed reading in response to a query seeking divination, farsight or insight through this pattern.

The Creation of the World

This method of laying out cards (ritual pattern making) is based upon the mystical cosmology contained in the *Vita Merlini* and the *Prophecies*. It is similar in many ways to the popular Celtic Cross method of pattern making, for both derive from the Wheel of Life, Circled Cross or Elemental cosmology/psychology of esoteric tradition. The symbolism is based upon a cycle or relationship of four rings (modes of energy/consciousness) united by a fifth representing unity or spirit and truth.

　　The layout uses nine or ten cards (see Figure 19). The order of laying out and turning up the cards is as follows.

1　*Centre:* Origin and seed of the query.
2　*Air:* New beginnings and energies of change. Power of Life.

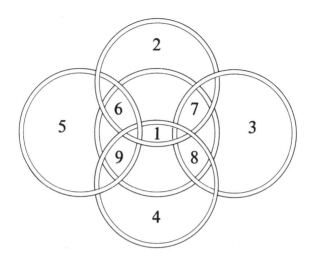

Figure 19: The Creation of the World

Original Powers

1 Origin and seed of query. TRUTH.
2 New beginnings and changes. LIFE.
3 Source of maximum energy or potential. LIGHT.
4 Nourishes, strengthens and purifies. LOVE.
5 Manifestation or outcome. LAW.

Archetypical personae

6 *Merlin:* Insight or prophetic awareness (spiritual influence).
7 *Guendoloena:* Positive emotions (lover).
8 *Ganieda:* Intellect, rational thought (sister, enabling influence).
9 *Rhydderch:* Outer activity.

3   *Fire:* Maximum source of energy within the query situation. Power of Light.
4   *Water:* Means of nourishing, purifying and maturing. Power of Love.
5   *Earth:* Manifestation or outcome of the query; form and definition of energies involved; may indicate opposing or balancing forces tending towards stabilization or resistance. Power of Law.

(Further attributes may be built through meditation upon the Fourfold Cross or Wheel of Life.)

Personae

To the basic fivefold pattern we may add four *personae*, described in the *Vita*, having parallels in various Trumps, and also found in variant forms as Court cards throughout tarot.

6   *Merlin:* Male anabolic energies/consciousness in spiritual or inner dimensions. Transcendent awareness.
7   *Guendoloena:* Female anabolic energies/consciousness in Nature. The power of positive emotions and sexuality.
8   *Ganieda:* Female catabolic energies/consciousness. The power of the intellect, serving higher consciousness and cultural or human development.
9   *Rhydderch:* Male activity manifesting in the outer world.

Thus the four *personae* represent broad images of energies, but may also stand for human individuals, depending on the cards that appear in their positions and the nature of the reading.

6   *Merlin:* Prophetic and higher consciousness.
7   *Guendoloena* (the wife of Merlin and polar 'sister' of Rhydderch): Emotional and sexual energies.

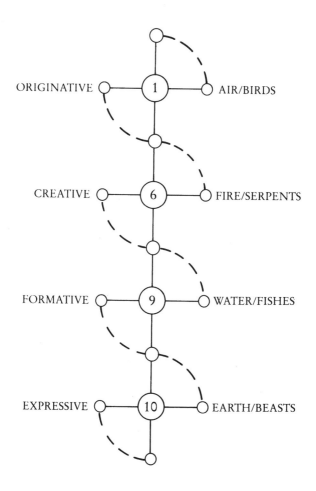

Figure 20: The Court Cards and the Four Modes

8 *Ganieda* (the sister of Merlin and wife of Rhydderch): All harmonious powers of the mind.

9 *Rhydderch* (a mighty king): Worldly matters of all sorts.

The *personae* complement the Elements defined by cards appearing in the basic fourfold pattern and stand at the Cross-Quarters, squaring the Circle by adding the human Elemental psyche to the natural and superhuman powers. It is worth noting that this layout is summarized completely in the Trump card The World or Universe, where the Elements and Worlds are defined, and the human modes of consciousness or *personae* are fused into one androgynous figure.

The four *personae* also correspond to a certain extent to the 1st–6th Spheres upon the Tree of Life, or levels within any one individual consciousness.

Finally a tenth card may be drawn (if required) as a summation of the entire matter; this is placed over the first card in the centre of the pattern. Paradoxically, this last card also represents The Fool, and may reveal surprise elements in the query situation or within its resolution.

The Ferryman

Despite connections between Merlin and King Arthur in fiction, there is no doubt that Merlin legends (as preserved in dated sources) pre-date Arthurian material. In the major Merlin sources there is little connecting Merlin and Arthur, and the Merlin story cycle may be completed without any Arthurian lore. In the works of Geoffrey of Monmouth, who began the popular restoration of Arthur in medieval literature, Merlin and Arthur hardly meet, though their relationship was soon to be developed by authors who elaborated upon lore set out by Geoffrey.

But in Geoffrey's *Vita Merlini* there is an important scene described, almost as an aside, in which Merlin and the bard Taliesin remind one another of the Fortunate Isle, ruled by the priestess or goddess Morgen. They carried the wounded Arthur to this magical Otherworld island for his cure by Morgen, who was skilled in therapeutic arts (see our Trump The Priestess). This curious scene, reflecting a Celtic tradition of kingship and the Otherworld, is the source for later developments of the relationship between Arthur and Merlin, and the theme of the wounded Arthur being carried to the Otherworld, Avallach or Avalon for restoration.

Merlin and Taliesin are steered to the Fortunate Isle by a mysterious ferryman Barinthus who is a mythical figure related to ancient sea gods and to the important role of psychopomp or Otherworld guide for souls of the dead or initiates. Thus, we have a significant grouping in the legend: *Merlin/Taliesin/Arthur/Barinthus/Morgen*. This grouping is reminiscent of similar relationships or structures that run through tarot in general, and may be used for meditation, farsight and insight, as shown in our Figure 21.

The basic *personae* may be interpreted as follows, with each one forming the basis for a position within a card layout.

Figure 21: The Ferryman

(From the legend of King Arthur in the *Vita Merlini*.)

1 *King Arthur:* Wounded *persona* or lame Fisher King.
2 *Taliesin:* Bard of knowledge.
3 *Merlin:* Prophet of future potential.
4 *Barinthus:* Mysterious Ferryman of the soul.
5 *Morgen:* Feminine power of redemption, transformation, therapy.

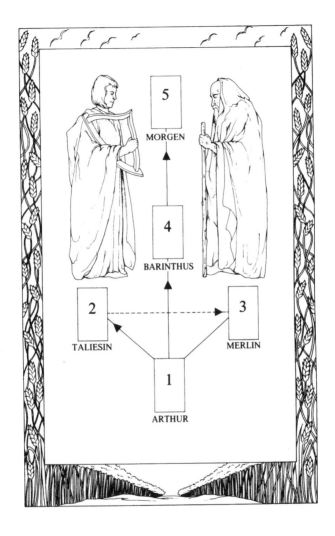

1 Indicates the querent's true nature/question/problem.

2 Reveals an initiatory rational analysis and answer (or a person who embodies such qualities).

3 Reveals an intuitive prophetic answer (or a person who may embody such an answer).

4 Symbolizes the power of movement towards balance, resolution, inner truth.

5 Indicates the outcome in terms of transformation and inner rebirth.

1 *Arthur* (The Wounded King, who is to be restored): represents the personality, which is a wounded, distorted image of our true inner self or spirit. Thus, this position reveals the inquirer's question, problem or difficulty. It will also suggest the true inner nature of a situation or sources of internal conflict or wounding.

2 *Taliesin* (The Bard of Knowledge, who teaches cosmology and traditional lore): represents intellectual and initiatory knowledge; reveals mental analytical aspects of the query, and may indicate the means towards solving any problems.

3 *Merlin* (The Prophet or Wild Man): represents intuitive emotional and poetic insights or inspiration; primal responses or magical transformations within a query situation. Indicates unusual or unexpected solutions to any problems.

4 *Barinthus* (The Otherworld Ferryman who enables the Wounded King to travel towards healing): the power of movement, resolution of situations, means whereby beneficial change may be achieved. May also indicate means of access to deep energies of change on a spiritual transformative level. Barinthus 'knows well the ways of sea and stars' (*Vita Merlini*), thus may work on an unconscious

collective level (the sea) or on a transpersonal spiritual level (the stars). His route is across the Middle Pillar or Spindle of the Worlds, from the Earth to the stars.

5   *Morgen* (The Priestess or Power of Redemption and Healing): represents the outcome of a situation or query, the point or person or inner state upon which the entire matter depends for its answer, just as the Wounded King depends upon Morgen for his ultimate healing.

Each of these five positions may be given emphasis by the presence of Trumps which relate either positively or negatively to the legendary *personae* described above. Thus a Spindle or *Axis Mundi* Trump (Moon, Sun, Star) on the position of Barinthus will indicate a strong mediating motivating factor of change, ranging from the Lunar to Stellar Worlds accordingly. By consulting our master key of the Trumps upon the Tree of Life (Figure 2) the reader can establish such relationships; it is useful in the early stages of development in tarot work to write out lists of such correspondences and learn them by heart. A typical preliminary list might read as follows, though this is not definitive:

1   *Arthur:* typified by The Fool/The Emperor/more subtly by The Hanged Man.
2   *Taliesin:* typified by The Magician/The Chariot/more subtly by The Innocent (Hierophant).
3   *Merlin:* typified by The Guardian/The Hermit.
4   *Barinthus:* typified by the three Spindle Trumps/Temperance.
5   *Morgen:* typified by The Priestess/The Empress/Strength.

Thus the polar opposites are:

1   The World/Death (*Arthur*).
2   The Priestess/The Lovers (*Taliesin*).
3   The Empress/The Innocent (The Hierophant) (*Merlin*).
4   The Three Wheels or threshold Trumps of Fortune, Justice and Judgement (*Barinthus*).
5   The Magician/The Guardian/The Blasted Tower (*Morgen*).

All 22 Trumps are included in the above basic correspondences. There is no implication that the two sets listed are 'good' or 'bad', only that they have a polar relationship. Meditation upon the meaning of each Trump and its relationships with other Trumps will gradually open out an understanding of their meaning when they appear in the highlighted or significant positions listed above.

Further Reading

Geoffrey of Monmouth, *The History of the Kings of Britain*. Various translations and editions.

Stewart, R. J., *The Complete Merlin Tarot* (The Aquarian Press, London, 1992).

—, *The Way of Merlin* (The Aquarian Press, London, 1991).

—, *The Prophetic Vision of Merlin and The Mystic Life of Merlin* (Penguin, Arkana, London, 1986) (in single volume, 1992). (These books analyse and comment upon the original Merlin texts of Geoffrey of Monmouth.)